EMBRACING THE TIGER

D1606301

THE EFFECTIVENESS DEBATE AND THE COMMUNITY COLLEGE

John E. Roueche
Laurence F. Johnson
Suanne D. Roueche
& Associates

Copyright 1997 The American Association of Community Colleges

Printed in the U.S.A.

Published by the Community College Press, a division of the
American Association of Community Colleges
One Dupont Circle, NW
Suite 410
Washington, DC 20036
(202) 728-0200

ISBN 0-87117-306-9

It is with great admiration of his love and respect for the power of higher education to positively affect the human condition, and with sincere regret for his early passing, that we dedicate this book to

ERNEST L. BOYER

Past President
Carnegie Foundation for the Advancement of Teaching

We remain strongly influenced by his fundamental belief in the obligation of our colleges to build a better world for the next generation.

Contents

Preface

Winston Churchill once observed that the world's dictators were riding to and fro on the backs of tigers from which they dared not dismount and that the tigers were getting hungry (*While England Slept*, 1938). Substitute colleges for dictators, and the current situation is accurately portrayed. Faced with declining resources, increased demands for services, and accelerated criticism by policy makers, legislators, students, and parents, colleges can no longer ignore a very public disaffection. Criticism of colleges' concerns for the current and future needs of their constituents, further fueled by their lukewarm responses to calls for greater accountability and improved institutional effectiveness measures, has brought them to a critical juncture. Colleges can either seriously attend to the wake-up calls being made by accrediting agencies, legislators, and the public—and respond in sincere, timely, and positive ways—or they can look forward to more stringent and more intrusive measures than currently exist. They must either embrace the effectiveness tiger or be eaten by it!

During this last decade, public inquiries into what colleges say they will do, what they actually do, and how well they do it have become increasingly more heated. Declining confidence in the value of a college degree, based primarily on graduates' preparedness levels, has increased the public's concern that higher education may no longer be a wise investment of time, energy, and money. Colleges are being asked to prove that they are responsible recipients of public funds and worthy recipients of the public trust. Critics and supporters alike remark that colleges can only prove themselves responsible and worthy by moving beyond what is currently required. They must not only respond to the letter of the law or of the policy regarding accountability and effectiveness; they must embrace both as opportunities to define more clearly who they are and to describe more specifically the value they add to their students and their communities.

At least this is the situation that current literature described for us. Uncomfortable with the general and widespread assessment that a majority of colleges were ignoring, by various degrees, serious demands for demonstration of accountability and effectiveness, we wanted to take a closer look at the state-of-the-art, at actual behaviors, and determine for ourselves if and how colleges were responding. The literature documents well at least a decade of attention to college performance—accrediting agencies revising their standards to include institutional effectiveness measures, national task forces investigating the pervasive decline in confidence in the value of a college degree, state legislatures and coordinating boards establishing effectiveness policies, and notable observers and researchers maintaining an intense and long-term scrutiny of and commentary about current accountability and effectiveness efforts. The current study was the result of our discomfort with this general assessment of college performance and response to public concerns.

We chose to bring currency to the discussion. In this report, we began by offering a bird's-eye perspective of some major issues and events that collectively create an appropriate backdrop for describing current practice. We took two approaches to describing current practice: a survey of 200 community college presidents from across the United States and Canada about current effectiveness issues and strategies, and a showcase of some community colleges that, by reputation, have been successful in comprehensively demonstrating institutional effectiveness. We believe that example is the best teacher, and, therefore, it was the stories of these leading colleges that we were particularly interested in telling.

A word about terminology is appropriate here. Throughout this book, we and the contributing authors use three terms almost synonymously; however, these terms—*accountability, institutional effectiveness,* and *assessment*—are not interchangeable and should not be construed as synonyms. They are, however, so intricately and intimately entwined in our collective discussions about colleges' responsibilities to their publics that the edges of their individual definitions are often blurred; and the particulars and subtleties of their individual definitions that describe their symbiotic relationships are often stretched or ignored completely in the interest of making a point or avoiding repetition. At the risk of oversimplification, we offer these broad definitions that can be fairly consistently applied to each term as it is used in the following chapters: *accountability* is the act of being responsible to various publics external to the college for implementation of its mission; *institutional effectiveness* is an internal strategy for planning and evaluating that generates data by which the college can determine if it is matching its performance to its purpose; and *assessment* expands the effectiveness strategy by determining the degree to which the college is meeting preset performance standards. In Chapter 2, we explain our decision to use the term *institutional effectiveness* to identify the concept we investigated in our national survey and the concept about which we asked our authors to write. In fact, after the study was completed, we agreed that institutional effectiveness as a phenomenon can legitimately be identified as the engine that propels colleges toward identifying appropriate assessment strategies that, through implementation, will provide viable and sufficient evidence of institutional accountability.

Our intent was to provide, by survey findings and by practical examples, a current snapshot of what many observers and researchers have labeled the institutional effectiveness movement. In Chapter 1, "Focusing on the Problem: Accountability and Institutional Effectiveness in the Community College," John Roueche, Katherine Boswell, and Suanne Roueche briefly draw out the imperatives that provide the current impetus for serious and aggressive college responses to public demands for improved institutional accountability, effectiveness policies, and assessment strategies; and sketch out the most common and controversial issues in the institutional effectiveness debate.

In Chapter 2, "Surveying Institutional Effectiveness in North American Community Colleges," Larry Johnson reviews the major goals of this study, describes the various strategies for achieving them—including the construction of the survey instrument and the selection of the contributing authors— and reviews the major findings from the survey results. He provides an informative prelude for the following contributed chapters that focus on individual strategies in current use among representative colleges with documented successes.

Chapters 3 through 9 are contributed chapters. We invited seven college presidents to tell their stories, to feature and highlight programs and practices at their colleges that defined, described, and evaluated specific effectiveness strategies. As we suspected, their collective chapters would represent a broad array of diverse strategies. We chose not to take a "best practices" approach to this showcase; rather, we wanted to feature a mix of colleges—large and small, urban and rural, with well-established and less-well-established models. An important component of each chapter is the final section in which each author discusses in some detail the lessons learned from the experiences described.

We wanted to paint the contemporary effectiveness landscape. While each of these contributions is easily a stand-alone representative of successful current practice, we saw important relationships among their messages and so arranged the chapters to best draw out some of the more common threads of the effectiveness tapestry. In truth, they could have been arranged in a variety of ways; their stories share so many common features. However, we trust that the transitions we provide between each of these seven chapters, and the framework in which we discuss the content of their messages in the final chapter, will help the reader bring some organization to this enormous bounty of information.

In the first of the contributed chapters, Chapter 3, "Seizing the Opportunity of Institutional Effectiveness," Jim Hudgins, president, and Starnell Williams, vice president for advancement, at Midlands Technical College (SC), document the college's 10-year journey towards refining the process that succinctly measures its impact on students and community. They illustrate how Midlands uses institutional effectiveness data to define the college mission and describe the achievement of that mission. Examples of current institutional practice illustrate the significant improvements the college has made in its teaching and learning process.

Chapter 4, "Productivity and Effectiveness at the Community College of Denver," describes another 10-year journey toward the pursuit of demonstrable effectiveness. Byron McClenney, president of CCD, describes the comprehensive process that currently drives planning throughout the institution—an annual cycle of activities that link vision, projections, and strategies; that includes all members of the CCD family; and that shares progress data with the community. He observes that in refining a successful approach to linking accountability and planning, the college family has created a tradition of planning for improvements and annually raising the bar by which success is measured.

In Chapter 5, "Effective Stewardship: Making the Case for Measuring Outcomes and Accountability," Pat McAtee, president, Cowley County Community College (KS), describes the complex issues and diverse activities that helped design and implement the college's institutional effectiveness model. This custom-designed model, based on the philosophy of total quality management and continuous process improvement, began with a review of the college mission and over the long-term included serious involvement with representatives of local business and industry, the community, and other colleges.

Chapter 6, "Developing an Institutional Effectiveness Model: Continuous Quality Improvement at Work," describes a college's embrace of the principles of continuous quality improvement. Walter Bumphus, president of Brookhaven College (TX), uses current examples to illustrate the implementation of the model and processes the college uses to plan, implement, and assess outcomes—including cross-functional teams, broad-based and fact-based planning, and systematic project team development. Recent outcome data document that current approaches to providing cost-effective service to varied constituencies in a mass customization process are working successfully. The implementation of CQI principles at the classroom level is a special component of this model.

In Chapter 7, "The Baltimore Phoenix," Jim Tschechtelin, president of Baltimore City Community College (MD), weaves a poignant tale of a college's death and rebirth through legislative action, the accompanying mandate for change, and the promise of a swift and certain institutional death if appropriate progress was not achieved in a time frame that by any standards appeared to be "mission impossible." Board policy defined the "bottom line" and identified the key indicators by which BCCC would measure the results of its efforts to be reborn. Tschechtelin illustrates how substantive change in quality is possible with clear goals, measurement of results, and high-performance people with positive mental attitudes.

In Chapter 8, "Seeking Quality at Humber College Through a Process for Transformation," Robert Gordon, president of Humber College of Applied Arts and Technology (Ontario) succinctly describes diverse stakeholders' perspectives about accountability issues, inputs, outputs, and outcomes. He outlines an "organic" approach to effectiveness that has focused on human resource and organizational development in a milieu of customer service, participation, innovation, and partnering for more than 10 years. The process he describes draws upon the perpetual renewal of human capital generated by a process for transformation that guides the college in developing measurable quality activities.

In Chapter 9, "A Shared Vision for Learning Outcome Improvements at Palomar College," George Boggs, president of Palomar College (CA), describes the college's major shift from a teaching to a learning paradigm. He credits the collective writing of new mission and vision statements that focused on student learning for a dramatic change in college direction. Outcome goals and measures are major components of an effectiveness model that targets measurable contributions to student learning and success. Operational and planning committees function with separate responsibilities that help clarify the contributions they can make to the overall governance of the college and help design the strategies by which the college can demonstrate its value to the public.

The final chapter, "The Tiger's Tale: A New Story for Community Colleges," revisits the wide-angle view taken in Chapter 2 and individualized in the seven contributed chapters. In this chapter, Roueche, Johnson, and Roueche address why colleges must respond quickly and positively to public questions and describe the major steps that have been taken thus far. Finally, the future of the institutional effectiveness movement is drawn out from the survey findings, various chapters, and authors' collective experiences. Some recommendations for improving current practice are made.

This study would not have been possible without the contributions of time and thoughtful effort by the presidents who responded to our survey on institutional effectiveness and the individuals whose chapters gave us reality by example. Many who responded to our survey were generous with information; they not only responded to our survey, but they frequently provided additional observations and numerous college documents that brought their answers to life. Each contributing author (and colleagues, in some instances), in addition to preparing thoughtful descriptions of effectiveness activities, accepted responsibility for proofing the final draft of his chapter after we had edited them for publication. Their enthusiasm and candor provided the energy and support that we enjoyed throughout the research and writing process. Our experiences with them will always be special recollections of this total effort.

Our special thanks go to Katherine Boswell, currently a graduate student in the Community College Leadership Program at The University of Texas at Austin. Katherine assumed responsibility for identifying and gathering appropriate and relevant background material about the effectiveness movement—issues, events, policies, research, and observations—and drafting the first working paper for Chapter 1 in partial fulfillment of her required graduate research internship. Her work on this project sparked a keen personal interest in effectiveness, and she is currently serving as project director of a two-year study of community college initiatives and performance, funded by Metropolitan Life Insurance Company and the Education Commission of the States. Katherine remained an active member of the editing team throughout the writing process.

As with numerous other research efforts for the CCLP and NISOD and dozens of other Community College Press publications, Sheryl Fielder, NISOD executive assistant, rode herd on draft copies of all chapters as we passed them back and forth during the writing, rewriting, and final editing stages—a monumental effort. She conducted the dreaded bibliographic checks, edited every chapter draft several times over with her meticulous eye for detail, and became proficient in manuscript production using the Quark software program required by the Community College Press but unfamiliar to all of us. Her special brand of quality is obvious throughout this book.

Having said all of that about two of our finest supporters in this process, we still assume total responsibility for all errors in this manuscript. The attention and care that Katherine and Sheryl brought to their assisting roles should not be judged by how well we ultimately fulfilled our own. It has been our intent that this effort will be of significant value to the readers for whom it is intended and, especially, for the colleges that we believe are the hope of our collective futures.

John E. Roueche
November, 1996   *Laurence F. Johnson*
                                                        Suanne D. Roueche

Chapter I

He who rides on a tiger
can never dismount.
—Chinese proverb

John E. Roueche
Katherine Boswell
Suanne D. Roueche
Community College Leadership Program
The University of Texas at Austin

FOCUSING ON THE PROBLEM: ACCOUNTABILITY AND EFFECTIVENESS IN THE COMMUNITY COLLEGE

Greater than the tread of mighty armies
is an idea whose time has come.
—Victor Hugo

American and Canadian colleges, founded on a philosophy of academic freedom and relative independence, have enjoyed substantial insulation from external pressures attempting to call them into account. Nonetheless, with some regularity over their more than 350-year history, the protective limits of this insulation have been tested by serious doubts raised about the quality of this admittedly complex and complicated business of educating for an informed citizenry and about the ability or the willingness of these institutions to improve upon this quality without external encouragement or mandate.

> To date, the academy's response to this condition has followed a predictable pattern. Externally, it is characterized by high-toned rhetorical protest and behind-the-scenes, no-holds-barred, political counterattack. Its chief internal feature, in turn, is diagnosis of the problem as short-term, residing less in the realm of performance than of public relations. (Ewell, 1994b, p. 25)

In reality, the academy has enjoyed a history that would support and encourage its belief that poor public relations—not performance—is the real problem. The cyclical nature of the love affair between institutions of higher education and the public can be documented historically. When the government and the people perceived colleges and universities as being "central to the progress of the nation," we saw increased access to higher education for GIs, for the baby boom generation, and for minorities and women. University research departments were established or enhanced and dedicated to improving defense capabilities, strengthening the war against disease, or building prosperity. During these periods, the public has tended to ignore the faults of colleges and universities and rallied behind them (Bok, 1992, p. 18). Yet, criticism and scrutiny have always returned in less pressing times.

There is strong evidence today that the remarkably persistent calls for accountability are not going to go away; rather, they will only grow louder as accrediting agencies, taxpayers, students, legislators, and other entities call for institutions of higher education to account for themselves. The accomplishments of higher education are in the distant past—they are "stale news." The academy must associate itself "once again with efforts to solve problems that really concern the people of this country" (Bok, 1992, p. 18). It cannot afford to ignore the evidence that "the rules of the accountability game have changed, as well as the ground on which it must be played" (Ewell, 1994b, p. 26). And, while colleges and universities are being asked questions that may seem unfair, they must be taken seriously. The questions require answers that reflect the academy's "commitment to academic values, self-examination, and change" (Marchese, 1994a, p. 4) and its dedication to regaining the "perception of integrity" historically bestowed upon it by the public and which now must be "earned back again by example and right action" (Ewell, 1994b, p. 26).

What Is the Problem?

The overarching problem is that the North American public's love affair with its institutions of higher education has come to an end; at the very least, the friendship has cooled. And, it is clear that community colleges, in particular, are at the most critical juncture of their lives. With "no ivy-covered walls behind which to shelter" (Ewell, 1994a, p. 73) and in the face of more external scrutiny and criticism than they have experienced to date, they are challenged not only to meet the goals set in their mission statements, but to prove that they have done so to the satisfaction of an unbelievably diverse mix of critics and judges. At this juncture, they can either cling, with tremendous peril, to self-absorbed beliefs that they are doing all they can, as well as they can, to serve their students and communities, and need not respond with enthusiasm to these challenges; or they can embrace the current press for comprehensive assessment and evaluation of their efforts with clarity of focus and documentable fervor. Critics contend that as a body politic, community colleges have done little more than study appropriate responses to demands for assessment, perhaps hoping they will go away or turn out to be far less threatening than they now appear. Those who are less critical, and those who by experience know firsthand about community colleges that are successfully strengthening their embrace, contend that colleges have taken the demands seriously and, if not currently responding appropriately, then are in the process of doing so.

The problems associated with increased scrutiny and pressure for change are exacerbated by the reality that despite years of discussion and external pressure, especially intense during the last decade, we just do not know the extent to which colleges have embraced comprehensive assessment and evaluation of their efforts. Do community colleges continue to see this as a "public relations" problem, or are they undertaking the kinds of changes that will ensure they remain responsive to their students' and communities' needs? The challenges posed by current questions about accountability and institutional effectiveness are literally lines drawn in the sand. Higher education and the public stand on either side.

Assessment Is Not a New Idea

Assessing or measuring the effectiveness of colleges and universities, programs, and services is a notion that is as old as higher education itself. In the U.S., it can be traced to the seventeenth century when Massachusetts Governor John Winthrop visited Harvard University to examine its first graduating class (Harcleroad, 1980). Colleges and universities implemented significant curricular change following the Revolution, reportedly after older students—many of whom had served in the Continental Army—pushed for reforms to move universities away from the classics to more practical subjects, and reforms continued well into the 1820s. The Morrill Act of 1862 provided support for publicly supported colleges and universities that had strong programs in the agricultural and mechanical arts—and was, perhaps, "the first major intersection of higher learning and national public policy" (Ewell, 1994b, p. 26). With the increasing numbers of publicly supported institutions, regional accrediting agencies were established (Sims, 1992), followed by the establishment of various programmatic accreditation entities and state accrediting bodies (Harcleroad, 1980). Clearly, whether or not the charters of these entities implicitly or explicitly stated that it was their intent to assess institutions' effectiveness and determine whether or not their missions were being fulfilled, it is apparent that this intent was a major, if not a primary goal (Young and Chambers, 1980).

As student populations grew, there were documentable complaints of too few assessment measures and a significant lack of a coherent and rigorous curricula (Resnick and Goulden, 1987; Sims, 1992). Federally funded programs and initiatives such as those provided by the Veterans Administration, the GI Bill, Pell grants, and student loans, along with other subsidies and direct funds to higher education, increased the demands of entities outside education for review of programs and overall accountability (Hauptman,

1991). Actions of the federal courts have resulted in decisions that have further involved the federal government in national higher education policy.

All projections indicate that the current, significant increases in college enrollments nationwide will continue (McClenney, 1994). The current 14.4 million students enrolled in colleges and universities are projected to grow to 16.4 million over the next decade (Dart, 1996). Projections by the Western Interstate Commission for Higher Education (WICHE) suggest that public high school graduating classes will increase by more than 34 percent between 1992 and 2009 (Finney, 1994)."With more than half of today's high school graduates headed to college, more people than ever before in our history are involved in higher education [and] have...more opportunity to criticize" (Cartwright, 1992, p. 14).

Increasing criticism and negative public opinion of education in general (and higher education in particular) and escalating expectations and demands in the face of rising costs and shrinking funds have continued to fuel scrutiny and calls for assessment (Ewell, 1994b; Halpern, 1987; Marchese, 1994a; and McGuinness, 1992).

Demands and Pressures on Community Colleges

In the U.S., after years of declining college entrance exam scores, the publication of *A Nation at Risk* (National Commission on Excellence in Education, 1983) chastened the American public education system for allowing "mediocre educational performance" (p. 5). Growing concerns about America's ability to compete in a global market turned even more serious attention of the public, elected officials, and accreditors to the issues of educational quality. Similar debates raged in provincial capitals across Canada.

In 1982, the Council on Postsecondary Accreditation (which at that time coordinated the activities of all accrediting agencies) directed institutions and programs to conduct "periodic self-evaluation seeking to identify what the institution does well, determining the areas in which improvement is needed, and developing plans to address needed improvements." One of the first bodies to respond was the Southern Association of Colleges and Schools (SACS) when, in 1986, it identified "institutional effectiveness" as a criterion of equal weight with the more traditional institutional process criteria, choosing that term, rather than the term "outcomes," to avoid the numerous negative connotations that "outcomes" would revive in the minds of many educators (Ewell, 1993). In the U.S., more than 90 percent of the states and all six regional accrediting agencies have instituted policies that require colleges and universities to adopt an institutional accountability or assessment plan in one form or another (El-Khawas, 1992). The Joint Commission on Accountability Reporting's (JCAR) technical report and conventions manual (1996) defines and describes the details of achieving national uniformity in accountability reporting. In Canada, there are no external accrediting agencies, but provincial governments across the nation are developing a variety of processes to hold educational institutions accountable.

Calls for major improvements in undergraduate education came with Bennett's *To Reclaim a Legacy* (1984), Bloom's *The Closing of the American Mind* (1987), and Smith's *Killing the Spirit* (1990). Amid the charges of poor instruction, hence less than adequate training of America's workforce, were concerns that taxpayers had been throwing good money at bad institutions (Finifter, Baldwin, and Thelin, 1991).

The responses to such charges from the educational community acknowledged the responsibility of higher education. The National Institute of Education's *Involvement in Learning* (1984) recommended that "colleges establish and maintain high standards of student and institutional performance" and measure their results "against...clearly and publicly articulated standards of performance" (p. 3). In 1985, the American Association of Colleges' *Integrity in the College Curriculum* declared that "colleges themselves must be held responsible for developing evaluations that the public can respect"(p. 33).

In 1986, the National Governors' Association issued *Time for Results* and called for colleges to measure what students were and were not learning. These reports argued for a more proactive role for state authorities in higher education based on a new conception of public accountability as "return on investment." That report, coupled with *Transforming the State Role in Improving Undergraduate Education* (Education Commission of the States, 1986) created expectations of large-scale standardized testing. Many states initially proposed such testing; the difficulty of identifying standardized examinations that would meet varied needs proved daunting, however, and most states decided to adopt a more individualized approach.

Reform efforts within the community college movement gained international attention with *Building Communities: A Vision for a New Century* (Commission on the Future of Community Colleges, 1988), prepared by a panel of community college leaders under the auspices of the American Association of Community and Junior Colleges (AACJC). This panel, the Futures Commission, pronounced that community colleges, "above all others, should expect the highest performance in each class and be creative and consistent in *the evaluation of results* [emphasis added]" (p. 25).

In 1989, President George Bush convened all 50 governors in Charlottesville, Virginia, for a National Education Summit. The National Goals 2000 project included a key objective for higher education: "The proportion of college graduates who demonstrate an advanced ability to think critically, communicate effectively, and solve problems will increase substantially" (National Education Goals Panel, 1995, p. 119). The Goals Panel recommended a sample-based, national assessment system to measure progress; while considerable preliminary work was undertaken by the

National Center on Education Statistics, funding was not appropriated by Congress, and national standards have yet to be established (Barton and Lapointe, 1995).

In June 1990, the Commission on the Skills of the American Workforce issued *America's Choice: High Skills or Low Wages!*, a report which as its centerpiece recommended that "by age 16 all students (both the college-bound and non-college-bound) should be expected to meet a new standard of educational performance" (p. 8). In 1991, the Secretary's Commission on Achieving Necessary Skills followed with "What Work Requires of Schools: A SCANS Report for America 2000," which began exploring the skills that should be included in an examination system to test job readiness. Worried about the rising rates of student loan defaults, the federal Office of Management and Budget (OMB) also got into the standards act. The 1990 Omnibus Budget Reconciliation Act included new legislative requirements that any student applying for federal aid who did not possess a high school diploma or its equivalent must first pass a test to demonstrate his or her "ability to benefit" from postsecondary education: "Without a word of debate, the federal government [was] in the business of setting national minimum standards through a test-approval process" (Edgerton, 1991, p. 9). Ernest L. Boyer, as president of the Carnegie Foundation for the Advancement of Teaching, observed that American citizens wanted evidence that the $180 billion annual investment in education was paying off and that "more than 60 percent of Americans surveyed...favor national standards, a national curriculum, and national tests for students" (1991, p. 190).

In 1993, the Wingspread Group on Higher Education, a panel of 16 leaders from education and business, assembled to address the question: "What does society need from higher education?" This panel wrote an "open letter to those concerned with the American future" and appended a collection of 32 essays addressing the topic by individuals representing diverse social, professional, and economic perspectives. A concern reminiscent of that in *A Nation at Risk* was expressed in this similarly influential document, *An American Imperative*:

> A disturbing and dangerous mismatch exists between what American society needs of higher education and what it is receiving. Nowhere is the mismatch more dangerous than in the quality of undergraduate preparation provided on many campuses. The American imperative for the 21st century is that society must hold higher education to much higher expectations or risk national decline. (p. 1)

From discussions during a 1994 Wingspread conference on accountability, Marchese, editor of *Change*, observed:

The legislators and board members who press for accountability increasingly embrace notions of continuous improvement, collective responsibility, customer focus, and management by fact; to them, colleges and universities...look like organizational left-behinds that can't be very interested in quality...and don't listen sympathetically or well enough to the paying publics we're supposed to serve. (1994a, p. 4)

Ewell, longtime researcher and observer of accountability and institutional effectiveness measures, suggests that higher education is in a state of crisis—faced with accusations that its accrediting systems and self-evaluations are inadequate and self-serving, and that widespread abuse, collusion, mismanagement, and outright fabrication are common (1994b). The U.S. Congress' hearings on scientific fraud and financial malpractice in the use of research funds, best-selling books accusing universities of political conformity, and news magazines and newspapers making front-page stories of enormous tuition increases are contributing factors to the erosion of public trust—"the public has finally come to believe quite strongly that our institutions...are not making the education of students a top priority" (Bok, 1992, p. 15); "[w]e know a lot about how smart our students are when they arrive, but we know very little about how much they have learned by the time they leave" (p. 16).

Criticisms like these have hurt more than the image of higher education. U.S. and Canadian colleges and universities have experienced deep reductions during the 1990s (Jaschik, 1991). In 1993, "for the first time on record," there was an absolute decline in dollars provided to American colleges and universities (Hines and Higham, 1996)—from 14 percent of total general fund spending in 1990, to 12.6 percent in 1993 (Gold, 1995). In Ontario, Canada's largest province, the provincial government imposed an overall budget cut of 14 percent on all colleges for the 1996-97 fiscal year. Indications are that "several years of shrill public criticism of higher education's performance...have played a part" (Breneman, 1995, p. B-1).

State and Provincial Responses
State and provincial governments, with higher education agencies, have traditionally monitored standards by setting admissions criteria and institutional licensing or accreditation requirements. But increasing concerns about educational quality have renewed the debate regarding the desirability of establishing a common set of performance standards for all college graduates, or all sophomores, or other specified groups (McClenney, 1994).

A consequence of recent federal "right to know" legislation has been a standardized national methodology for calculating and reporting common statistics on collegiate outcomes (Ewell, 1991). A new mechanism for accountability—a *USA Today* editorial viewed the State Postsecondary Review Entity (SPRE) as "a significant step in providing greater consumer protection for students pursuing a postsecondary education and in safeguarding the integrity of student and programs" (August 1994)

To effect significant improvements at the institutional level, states and provinces can change budgetary allocation processes to provide special funds for needed improvements which encourage successful performance. In 1990, the National Center for Postsecondary Governance and Finance reported that states had supported approximately $1.25 billion in incentive funding over the 1980s, in a variety of categorical, competitive, and mixed-category programs (Lively, 1992). In the 1960s and 1970s, most state and provincial governments adopted enrollment-driven funding formulas that were quite effective in accommodating growth. But the majority of these formulas concentrated on input measures that were readily quantifiable—for example, enrollments, faculty, or gross square footage, which did not account for increasing expectations and pressure to measure improvement in student learning and development (Ewell, 1986). Concern for meeting these qualitative requirements has encouraged the use of incentive funds, usually tied to performance on specific goals.

Performance funding is viewed differently by higher education agencies than by colleges and universities. Agencies set priorities that include obtaining evidence of institutional accountability, eliminating program duplication, and building regionally and nationally recognized centers of excellence, while maintaining relatively convenient access. These purposes are best served by common evaluation standards that apply to each institution and permit comparison of similar programs across institutions. Colleges and universities, however, prefer to establish local objectives and priorities that reflect their own unique mission and circumstances. They tend to view statewide or provincewide standards with apprehension because such measures invite public comparison of programs that may have been designed to meet different needs, and because of the competition factor that often exists between institutions (Banta, 1986).

Nonetheless, many states have already initiated incentives for the institutionalization of effectiveness measures. As early as 1979, Tennessee instituted a performance-based funding program using performance criteria applied to all publicly supported institutions of higher education. Initially, two percent of Tennessee's education and general budget was earmarked for the program, but in subsequent years that percentage has risen substantially. Since Tennessee instituted its incentive programs, numerous states and all the regional accrediting associations have called upon institutions to demonstrate their accountability for the use of public funds.

By 1989, some two-thirds of states in the U.S. had developed policies that included most of the following basic features:

- A requirement that each institution develop an explicit plan for assessment including statements of intended instructional outcomes, proposed methods for gathering evidence, and a proposed organizational structure
- Substantial institutional latitude in developing goal statements and in selecting or designing appropriate methods for gathering evidence
- Mandatory reporting of results to state authorities on a regular schedule, generally coincident with the state's budget cycle
- An expectation that institutions themselves would pay the costs of assessment (Virginia and Washington were prominent exceptions)
- Few real or immediate consequences for institutional compliance or the lack of it (exceptions here were Colorado, where accountability legislation allowed institutions to be penalized by up to 2 percent of their budgets if they were not in compliance, and Virginia)
- The general expectation that information resulting from local assessment programs would simultaneously induce campus-level change and fulfill growing state-level demands for accountability
- The expectation that results would eventually be helpful in developing state-level academic policies and in determining key areas of need for selective investment. (Ewell, 1993, pp. 344-345)

Colorado, Missouri, New Jersey, South Dakota, and Virginia have embarked on programs linking an institution's assessment of student outcomes to eligibility for incentive funds or other tangible awards (Ewell, 1988). Texas, Arkansas, Kentucky, South Carolina, and New Mexico associate funding with institutional reporting of such quantitative data as retention/graduation rates, placement of graduates, and for community colleges, rates of transfer to four-year institutions (Banta, Rudolph, Van Dyke, and Fisher, 1996).

Missouri and South Dakota have instituted senior-level testing programs, while Arkansas, Florida, and Texas have rising junior exams (Barton and Lapointe, 1995). The Texas Academic Skills Program (TASP) and Florida's College Level Academic Skills Test (CLAST) measure basic skill mastery at the lower division or sophomore level (Bogue and Saunders, 1992). Kentucky is requiring efficiency reports on the use of classroom space, faculty workloads, time and credits needed to graduate with various degrees, and passing rates on professional exams taken by graduates, while South Carolina now requires public colleges and universities to annually report such information as graduation rates, job placement rates, balance of graduate students and faculty members teaching lower division courses, minority enrollment, and the number and percentage of accredited programs (Lively, 1992). A series of bills was introduced in the 1996 California legislative session addressing performance accountability and innovation, including a bill that would establish the Higher Education Performance Challenge Act to support and encourage innovation in postsecondary educational institutions ("Performance, Accountability and Innovation Bills Introduced," 1996).

Issues in the Current Environment

Assessment creates particular challenges for community colleges. "Far more than any sector, the proof of effectiveness for the community college lies in the judgments of those whom the institution is bound to serve—students, employers, other colleges and universities, and members of the local community" (Ewell, 1994, p. 73). While community colleges have been in the forefront of assessment efforts, it is a tremendously challenging environment in which to demonstrate success. "Enormous diversity in student abilities and backgrounds, relatively slim databases about student characteristics and activities, and, above all, the variety of ways in which students experience instruction often preclude the use of techniques 'proven' in other settings" (Ewell, 1994, p. 74). Many community college students are unwilling to engage in testing that will not benefit them directly; moreover, as a result of their commuting and work schedules, they are not always available for routine data collection.

Many faculty argue that the current wave of assessment requirements do not bode well for the quality of higher education in the future. By dividing the ends of education into measurable "outcomes," accountability attempts to conquer higher education's many complexities, redundancies, and contradictions; and whets government bureaucrats' appetites for measurement and control (Rogers, 1994). In a 1993 survey of 71 systems of governing bodies and state coordinating boards, 25 percent of the respondents said that issues related to faculty workload and productivity were very important. The same survey revealed that one of every four states has or is considering legislation on faculty workload issues (Finney, 1994).

Measuring institutional effectiveness. There are as many approaches to measuring effectiveness as there are colleges. Public perceptions of effectiveness change over time. Executive management information systems (Glover and Krotseng, 1993); student tracking systems (Palmer, 1990); levels of expenditure of institutional resources—politics, services, materials, dollars, and staff—in meeting constituency needs (Thompson, Alfred, and Lowther, 1987); and tying effectiveness to assessment, planning, budgeting, and resource allocation (Brown and Johnson, 1995) have been common discussions.

Hudgins argues that community colleges have been judged too often by university standards or very narrow criteria related to the transfer function. The problem has not been that the standards were too high, rather that they simply were not the appropriate standards (Hudgins, 1991, 1997). Community college leaders have long held that the two-year colleges have unique missions and should be judged by standards relevant to their mission.

In focus groups of business, political, and academic leaders convened in 1995 by the Education Commission of the States, participants identified desirable student outcomes for community colleges that included the following:

- Higher order, applied problem-solving abilities
- Enthusiasm for continuous learning
- Interpersonal skills, including communication and collaboration
- A strong sense of responsibility for personal and community action
- Ability to bridge cultural and linguistic barriers
- A well-developed sense of "professionalism" (pp. 6-7).

Institutional attributes that "ensure that the conditions for quality exist" include: student-centeredness; commitment to specific "good practices" in instruction; quality management practices; and efficiency and integrity of operations (pp. 7-8).

In 1994, the Community College Roundtable identified 13 core indicators which, while not totally comprehensive of every aspect of community college life, appear to capture the critical functions that reflect the community college mission. Each measure is accompanied by a description of how it is determined, potential sources of data, and additional measures that might be considered to ascertain effectiveness. Indicators include:

- Student goal attainment
- Persistence (fall to fall)
- Degree completion rates
- Placement rate in the workforce
- Employer assessment of students
- Number and rate who transfer
- Performance after transfer
- Success in subsequent, related coursework
- Demonstration of critical literacy skills
- Demonstration of citizenship skills
- Client assessment of programs and services
- Responsiveness to community needs
- Participation rate in service area (pp. 16-25).

Ewell recommends a series of appropriate assessment methods that meet the unique requirements of the community college environment:

- Develop longitudinal information on student experience and performance
- Carefully target special assessments of student performance

- Capitalize on collecting additional information at existing points of contact with students
- Develop better mechanisms for getting information to those who need it (1994a, pp. 83-86).

Ewell's suggestions, and those of the Community College Roundtable, are specifically designed to meet the unique needs of community colleges and the information derived from such processes can serve as significant catalysts for institutional renewal, especially if guided by the following key assessment principles:

- *Multiple measures* are critical because each may reflect different aspects of a given institution's condition or performance; therefore, "indexing" or "profiling" quality along numerous dimensions is appropriate.
- *Mixed measures* are important to address both *desired student outcomes and institutional attributes,* as well as a mix of *qualitative and quantitative measures* of performance.
- *Contextual data reporting* is necessary because it provides consumers with the opportunity to better understand and assess quality differences among institutions in relation to the context in which they operate.
- *Information about both absolute outcomes and the educational "value added"* by colleges and universities is important in reaching overall quality judgments....There should be some common meaning to a college degree in terms of basic skills, knowledge levels, and other "absolute" outcomes. But...different institutions vary widely in terms of academic preparation of students. Thus the "value added" by a community college, for example, would be different from (and might exceed) the valued added by an elite, four-year university. Both types of measures are important.
- *External sources* about performance are critical, not just to help ensure validity, but also to incorporate different perspectives. These should include the ratings and perceptions of people closely involved, such as students and employers.
- *Comparative measures* across institutions can be useful but only if comparisons are made among colleges and universities with similar missions and operating conditions. (Education Commission of the States, 1995, p. 8)

The accreditation process. The traditional means of certifying and enhancing quality in higher education has been through a set of self- and peer-review processes that when conducted according to the guidelines or requirements of the accrediting agency, result in accreditation. This process of assessing and maintaining quality through self-regulation is unique to the United States. Other countries traditionally have given the authority to establish and regulate national standards to national ministries of education (Semrow, Barney, Fredericks, Fredericks, Robinson, and Pfnister, 1992). But there have been deep concerns expressed about the quality assurance role provided by the six regional accrediting agencies. "In 1992, Congress came close to dropping accreditation as the eligibility trigger for federal student aid support; in 1993, the Council on Post Secondary Education folded; and in 1994, alarms went off about the Department of Education's proposed rule-making for accreditation" (Marchese, 1994b, p. 4). In January 1994, a newly formed National Policy Board for Higher Institutional Accreditation (NPB) agreed to pursue significant changes in the accreditation process, agreeing that steps must be taken to increase accreditation's credibility with and value to the public (Education Commission of the States, 1995). Working groups from within the higher education community were appointed to draft new accreditation guidelines and procedures that would establish a common set of baseline standards. However, despite promises and plans to reform accreditation, little has been accomplished.

The quality issue. Traditional measures of quality have considered the quantity of resources such as the number of books in the library, Ph.D.s on the faculty, or the selectivity of the student body. Other quality measures have included: accreditation processes, which are measures of goal achievement and improvement; rankings and ratings, which are tests of reputation; outcomes, which are performance results; licensures, which are various professional standards; program reviews, which focus on peer reviews; and follow-up studies, which measure client satisfaction (Bogue and Saunders, 1992).

The value-added approach to measuring quality has been a recurring and widely accepted concept and is considered to be even more important than measuring outcomes (Astin, 1985). The value-added criteria for quality is based on the assumption that it is the difference between the start and end of the educational process that is important, not just the start (input) or the end (output) itself—"true excellence lies in the institution's ability to affect its students and faculty favorably, to enhance their intellectual and scholarly development, and to make a positive difference in their lives" (pp. 60-61).

Current interest in public accountability has led to some efforts to adapt total quality management principles from the business world to higher education. American industry has developed quality principles in response to four motivating forces: "(1) survival in an increasingly competitive environment; (2) the escalation of the costs of doing business; (3) a trend to make organizations more accountable for their actions and outcomes; and (4) a blurring of the distinction between 'products' and 'services'" (Seymour, 1993,

p. 3). Higher education faces these same pressures. The fundamental issue is "How can we, as academic administrators, do a better job of managing quality into our campus operations?" (Seymour, 1993, p. 39)

Marchese identifies six key ideas of CQI/CPI that are relevant for colleges and universities; they are paraphrased here:

- *Customer focus.* The doctrine of customer focus forces everyone within the organization to get out of the cubbyholes they work in and talk with the "real people" they're serving. Too often organizations are run for the people who work in them.
- *Continuous improvement.* To reach ever higher performance levels every year, an organization needs to think systematically about the constant improvement of all processes that deliver value to its customers. Derek Bok, former President of Harvard remarked that—thousands of projects, task forces, foundation grants, and journal articles notwithstanding—the state of teaching and learning in higher education seems no better than it was 20 years ago.
- *Management by fact.* Continuous improvement implies that "quality" has to be specified and monitored. The use of data to keep track and improve is critical to the process.
- *Benchmarking.* Too often in our colleges and universities the same absence of ethic that constrains continuous improvement makes searching for "best practices" nonexistent. Most campuses have the ethic, "we're unique—it won't work here."
- *People.* A very important emphasis in the quality movement is people. If an organization is anxious to improve, it will see its people as its greatest resource. It does everything possible to give every employee the preparation, tools and initiative to contribute to corporate goals. In TQM, 85 percent of the problems that arise in the course of work are attributed to the organization's systems. Just 15 percent of the shortcomings are because of the individual failings of an employee.
- *Organizational structure.* Work should be organized around the needs and preferences of customers, not those of the corporation or its employees. American colleges are incredibly vertical and compartmentalized, like corporations were 10 years ago. (1993, pp. 10-13)

The adaptation of total quality efforts to higher education has not been without critics who observe: the metaphor of student-as-customer compromises the goals of education by defining the customer too narrowly, confusing short-term satisfaction with long-term learning, and insufficiently accounting for student teacher interactions (Schwartzman, 1995) and applying total quality initiatives to higher education problems may be too complex and complicated (Brigham, 1993).

Accountability of Colleges and Universities (Graham, Lyman, and Trow, 1995), issued by the Mellon Foundation, has identified quality as the primary concern in undergraduate education and urged each institution to recommit itself to teaching and learning, backing that commitment with candid reviews focusing on quality in individual academic units, conducted within a climate of self-inquiry. Increasingly, attention has centered on student outcomes, a significant change in focus from process and resource inputs traditionally used as measures of quality.

Conclusions

Twenty-five years ago, *Accountability and the Community College: Directions for the 70s* (Roueche, Baker, and Brownell, 1972), a monograph commissioned by the American Association of Junior Colleges (AAJC), pronounced educational accountability as "an idea whose time had come" (p. 1), recommended that colleges "define their own responsibilities" before others outside the institutions do; and prophesied that "[a]ccountability is inevitable because it is needed so desperately" (p. 8). Today, we can pronounce it more than an idea; rather, we can cite it as a reality, a significant feature of what many choose to describe as the institutional effectiveness movement. Colleges and universities must respond to its challenges of accountability and associated measures of institutional effectiveness because it is the right thing to do; and by so doing, they may help restore public faith in the profession and the academy. And, simultaneously, they must acknowledge the implicit threat of external intervention by state and federal agencies if they respond poorly or not at all.

Undoubtedly, the current "ideal times" have been made more complex and threatening by a plethora of present-day challenges, policies, and legislation that this chapter could not and did not attempt to fully describe or explain. "Real educational leadership" has its work cut out for the foreseeable future. Assessment will be a leadership challenge: "campus leaders, especially presidents [are] the people whose attitude toward public issues like assessment set the tone for their campuses' responses" (Edgerton, 1990, p. 4).

Community college leaders are being challenged to determine whether or not their institutions are fulfilling their missions and to identify viable alternatives, processes, and procedures by which they can measure institutional success. Internal and external pressures are converging as catalysts and incentives for colleges to assess the quality of their programs; more emphatically, they hint that time is running out. Former Colorado State Senator Al Meiklejohn, while a member of the Education Commission of the States, observed that it is "almost too late" for colleges to improve their quality by themselves. "Some know we need to talk about quality; others have circled the wagons," he said. "I'd like to see them talk about measuring quality," he added. "But if they can't, it may take legislation and financial pressure to do it" (Mercer, 1994, p. A-20).

Taxpayers, government officials, and accreditation associations have given colleges ample evidence, by their collective interests, legislative and policy statements, and actions, that escalating demands for educational accountability and increased scrutiny of the measures by which we will judge ourselves and by which others will judge us are in our collective futures to stay. However, there are grave signs that many colleges choose to turn a deaf ear and a blind eye to this future. Governor Roy Romer of Colorado, the 1994-95 chairman of the Education Commission of the States, articulated the state of this art:

> I continue to be amazed at the resistance I encounter to examining whether we can measure and report on effective learning at individual institutions and provide good information to inform consumers about their choices. I also continue to be amazed at the inability of policy makers and public leaders to create meaningful and useful accountability systems for higher education. Finally, I am amazed at how many people are content to rest on the laurels of the past and insist that our higher education institutions need not change because they are the best in the world. (Education Commission of the States, 1995, p. v)

The past is past. Colleges should and must be concerned about institutional effectiveness: "the comparison of the results achieved to the goals intended" (Ewell, 1983, p. 89); "matching performance to purpose" (Southern Association of Colleges and Schools, 1991, Section III); "a mindset that asks questions—good questions, hard questions, legitimate questions—about what and how much our students are learning" (Edgerton, 1990, p. 5); and "the process of articulating the mission of the college, setting goals, defining how the college and community will know when these goals are being met and using the data from assessment in an ongoing cycle of planning and evaluation" (Grossman and Duncan, 1989, p. 5).

Why must colleges be concerned? It is in their best self-interests; it will lay the foundations for future support. Those who support community colleges today will find it more and more difficult to support them in the future without authentic and documentable evidence that they aspire and succeed in providing the best service for students and communities. Legislators will continue to deny funding and squeeze the fiscal life from colleges that do not make substantive and honest efforts to comply with their demands for increased accountability and improved assessment. Finally, colleges should be concerned because the documentation of effectiveness is an idea whose time has come—legislators want it, taxpayers want it, students want it. Community colleges were intended to be responsive institutions from their earliest beginnings; providing students and taxpayers proof that they are accomplishing their missions is simply an expression of that responsiveness—and the right thing to do.

Are community colleges answering the call? Do they believe that they are doing all they can, as well as they can, to serve their students and communities, and need not respond with enthusiasm to these challenges; or have they embraced the current press for comprehensive assessment and evaluation of their efforts? As noted in the opening of this chapter, some critics contend that community colleges have spent their time studying appropriate responses to demands for assessment, and doing little else in the hope that the demands will disappear or be significantly reduced. Others contend that colleges have taken the demands seriously and are in the process of responding appropriately. Which group is right? The reality is that despite years of discussion and external pressure, especially intense during the last decade, we just do not know the extent to which colleges have embraced comprehensive assessment and evaluation of their efforts. Do community colleges continue to see this as a "public relations" problem, or are they undertaking the kinds of changes that will ensure they remain responsive to their students' and communities' needs?

Providing a definitive answer to these questions is a central purpose of this book, and the chapters that follow will accomplish that purpose on two levels. The first is an attempt to describe the landscape—to document the status of institutional effectiveness practices in North American two-year colleges—and in the process provide a broad-brush picture of what community colleges are measuring and what forces are influencing their decisions about the documentation of effectiveness. The second is to fill in the details—to provide the reader with practical examples of how individual colleges have answered the challenges of the effectiveness debate. The seven colleges featured include institutions large and small, inner city and rural, colleges with years of experience in documenting their success and colleges in the early stages of an uphill climb.

The overarching issues of the effectiveness movement—ever-greater competition for funds, the press of legislative, board, and taxpayer attentions, increased scrutiny and public criticism—will surface again and again as we turn to college responses, for they are an inseparable part of the debate. If one thing is clear from our examination of the issues, it is that institutional effectiveness is no paper tiger. It is real, and colleges can no longer hide behind a curtain of anecdotal data. The problem facing community colleges as many of them move into their third decade is not that they need to tell their story better; they need a better story to tell.

REFERENCES

American Association of Colleges. *Integrity in the College Curriculum: A Report to the Academic Community*. Washington, DC: American Association of Colleges, 1985.

Astin, A.W. *Achieving Education Excellence: A Critical Assessment of Priorities and Practices in Higher Education*. San Francisco: Jossey-Bass, 1985.

Banta, T.W., Rudolph, L.B., Van Dyke, J., and Fisher, H.S. "Performance Funding Comes of Age in Tennessee." *The Journal of Higher Education*, 1996, *67*, 23-45.

Banta, T.W. (ed.). *Performance Funding in Higher Education: A Critical Analysis of Tennessee's Experience*. Boulder, CO: National Center for Higher Education Management Systems, 1986.

Barton, P.E. and Lapointe, A. *Learning by Degrees: Indicators of Performance in Higher Education*. Princeton, NJ: Policy Information Center, Educational Testing Service, 1995.

Bennett, W. *To Reclaim a Legacy: A Report on the Humanities in Higher Education*. Washington, DC: National Endowment for the Humanities, 1984.

Bloom, A. *The Closing of the American Mind: How Higher Education Has Failed Democracy and Impoverished the Souls of Today's Students*. New York: Simon and Schuster, 1987.

Bok, D. "Reclaiming the Public Trust: How Universities and Colleges Need to Cope with a Public Lack of Confidence." *Change*, July/August 1992, 24, 12-19.

Bogue, E.G. and Saunders, R.L. *The Evidence for Quality*. San Francisco: Jossey-Bass, 1992.

Boyer, E. "The National Index: A Framework for State Accountability. *Vital Speeches*, January 1, 1991, *57*, 189-192.

Breneman, D.W. "Sweeping, Painful Changes." *The Chronicle of Higher Education*, September 8, 1995, B1-B2.

Brigham, S.E. "TQM: Lessons We Can Learn from Industry." *Change*, May/June 1993, *25*, 42-48.

Brown, B. and Johnson, R. "Integrating Assessment with Institutional Planning, Budgeting and Resource Allocation." Speech presented at AAHE Conference on Assessment and Quality, Boston, June 11, 1995.

Cartwright, C.A. "Reclaiming the Public Trust: A Look to the Future. *AAHE Bulletin*, June 1992, *44*, 14-16.

Commission on the Future of Community Colleges. *Building Communities: A Vision for a New Century*. Washington, DC: American Association of Community and Junior Colleges, 1988.

Commission on the Skills of the American Workforce. *America's Choice: High Skills or Low Wages!* Rochester, NY: National Center on Education and the Economy, 1990.

Community College Roundtable. *Community Colleges: Core Indicators of Effectiveness.* Washington, DC: American Association of Community Colleges, 1994.

Council on Postsecondary Accreditation (COPA). *Policy Statement on the Role and Value of Accreditation.* Washington, DC: Council on Postsecondary Accreditation, 1982.

Dart, B. "Tuition Is Less than You Think." *Austin American-Statesman,* September 26, 1996, D1, D7.

Edgerton, R. "National Standards Are Coming! National Standards Are Coming!" *AAHE Bulletin,* December 1991, *44,* 8-12.

Edgerton, R. "Assessment at Half-Time." *Change,* September/October 1990, 22 4-5.

Education Commission of the States. *Making Quality Count in Undergraduate Education: A Report for the ECS Chairman's "Quality Counts" Agenda in Higher Education.* Denver: Education Commission of the States, 1995.

Education Commission of the States. *Transforming the State Role in Undergraduate Education: Time for a Different View*8
Denver: Education Commission of the States, 1986.

El-Khawas, E. *Campus Trends Survey.* Washington, DC: American Council on Education, 1992.

Ewell, P.T. "Acting Out State-Mandated Assessment." *Change,* July/August 1988, *20,* 40-47.

Ewell, P.T. "The Assessment Movement: Implications for Teaching and Learning." In O'Banion, T. (ed.), *Teaching and Learning in the Community College.* Washington, DC: Community College Press, 1994a.

Ewell, P.T. "Back to the Future: Assessment and Public Accountability." *Change,* November/December 1991, *23,* 12-17.

Ewell, P.T. *Information on Student Outcomes: How to Get It and How to Use It.* Boulder, CO: National Center for Higher Education Management Systems, 1983.

Ewell, P.T. "A Matter of Integrity: Accountability and the Future of Self-Regulation." *Change,* November/December, 1994b, *26,* 24-29.

Ewell, P.T. "Performance Funding and Institutional Response: Lessons from the Tennessee Experience." In Banta, T.W. (ed.), *Performance Funding in Higher Education: A Critical Analysis of Tennessee's Experience.* Boulder, CO: National Center for Higher Education Management Services, 1986.

Ewell, P.T. "The Role of States and Accreditors in Assessment." In Banta, T.W. and Associates (eds.), *Making a Difference: Outcomes of a Decade of Assessment in Higher Education.* San Francisco: Jossey-Bass, 1993.

Finifter, D.H., Baldwin, R.G., and Thelin, J.R. (eds.). *The Uneasy Public Policy Triangle in Higher Education.* New York: American Council on Education, Macmillan Publishing Co., 1991.

Finney, J.E. "Tough Choices for Higher Education." *Spectrum: The Journal of State Government*, 1994, *67*, 24-30.

Glover, R.H. and Krotseng, M.V. (eds.). *Developing Executive Information Systems for Higher Education*. San Francisco: Jossey-Bass, 1993.

Gold, S. *The Fiscal Crisis of the States*. Washington, DC: Georgetown University Press, 1995.

Graham, P.A., Lyman, R., and Trow, M. *Accountability of Colleges and Universities*. New York: Andrew W. Mellon Foundation, 1995.

Grossman, G.M. and Duncan, M.E. *Indications of Institutional Effectiveness: A Process for Assessing Two-Year Colleges*. Columbus, OH: Center on Education and Training for Employment, 1989.

Harcleroad, F.F. "The Context of Academic Program Evaluation." In Craven, E.C. (ed.), *Academic Program Evaluation*. New Directions for Institutional Research No. 27. San Francisco: Jossey-Bass, 1980.

Halpern, D.F. (ed.). *Student Outcomes Assessment: What Institutions Stand to Gain*. New Directions for Higher Education No. 59. San Francisco: Jossey-Bass, 1987.

Hauptman, A.M. "Trends in the Federal and State Financial Commitment to Higher Education." In Finifter, D.H. et al. (eds.), *The Uneasy Public Policy Triangle in Higher Education*. New York: American Council on Education, Macmillan Publishing Co., 1991.

Hines, E.R. and Higham, J.R., III. *State Higher Education Appropriations 1995-96*. Denver: State Higher Education Executive Officers, 1996.

Hudgins, J.L. "Institutional Effectiveness: A Strategy for Institutional Renewal." *Occasional Paper: Southern Association of Community, Junior and Technical Colleges*, May 1991, *9*.

Hudgins, J.L. "Seize the Opportunity." *Celebrations*, February 1997.

Jaschik, S. "State Funds for Higher Education Drop in First Year: First Decline Since Survey Began 33 Years Ago." *The Chronicle of Higher Education*, November 6, 1991, A-1, A-38.

Joint Commission on Accountability Reporting (JCAR). *A Need Answered: An Executive Summary of Recommended Accountability Reporting Formats*. Washington, DC: American Association of State Colleges and Universities, 1996.

Lively, K. "Accountability of Colleges Gets Renewed Scrutiny from State Officials." *The Chronicle of Higher Education*, September 2, 1992, A-25.

Marchese, T. "Accountability." *Change*, November/December 1994a, *26*, 4.

Marchese, T. "Reinventing Accreditation" (editorial). *Change*, March/April 1994b, *26*, 4.

Marchese, T. "TQM: A Time for Ideas." *Change*, May/June 1993, *25*, 10-13.

McClenney, K.M. "Policy to Support Teaching and Learning." In O'Banion, T. (ed.), *Teaching and Learning in the Community College*. Washington, DC: Community College Press, 1994.

McGuinness, A.C., Jr. "Lessons from European Integration for U.S. Higher Education." Paper presented at the Eleventh Annual General Conference, Programme on Institutional Management in Higher Education, Organisation for Economic Development and Cooperation, Paris, September 1992.

Mercer, J. "Defining Public Expectations: State Group to Focus on College Quality." *The Chronicle of Higher Education*, July 13, 1994, A-20.

National Commission on Excellence in Education. *A Nation at Risk: The Imperative for Educational Reform*. Washington, DC: U.S. Department of Education, 1983.

National Education Goals Panel. *The National Education Goals Report: Building a Nation of Learners*. Washington, DC: U.S. Department of Education, 1995.

National Governors' Association, Task Force on College Quality. *Time for Results: The Governors' 1991 Report on Education*. Washington, DC: National Governors' Association, 1986.

National Institute of Education. *Involvement in Learning: Realizing the Potential of American Higher Education*. Report of the Study Group on the Conditions of Excellence in American Higher Education. Washington, DC: U.S. Government Printing Office, 1984.

Palmer, J. *Accountability Through Student Tracking: A Review of the Literature*. Washington, DC: American Association of Community and Junior Colleges, 1990.

"Performance, Accountability and Innovation Bills Introduced." *Capitol Report*. Sacramento, CA: Community College League of California, March 19, 1996.

Resnick, D.P. and Goulden, M. "Assessment, Curriculum, and Expansion: A Historical Perspective." In Halpern, D.F. (ed.), *Student Outcomes Assessment: What Institutions Stand to Gain*. New Directions for Higher Education No. 59. San Francisco: Jossey-Bass, 1987.

Rogers, P. "Accountability and the Ends of Higher Education." *Change*, November/December 1994, *26*, 16-21.

Roueche, J.E., Baker, G.A., III, and Brownell, R.L. *Accountability and the Community College: Direction for the 70's*. Washington, DC: American Association of Community and Junior Colleges, 1972.

Schwartzman, R. "Are Students Customers? The Metaphoric Mismatch Between Management and Education." *Education*, 1995, *116*, 215-222.

Secretary's Commission on Achieving Necessary Skills. *What Work Requires of Schools: A SCANS Report for America 2000*. Washington, DC: U.S. Department of Labor, June 1991.

Semrow, J.J., Barney, J.A., Fredericks, J., Fredericks, M., Robinson, P., and Pfnister, A.O. *In Search of Quality: The Development Status and Forecast of Standards in Postsecondary Accreditation*. New York: Peter Lang, 1992.

Seymour, D. *On Q: Causing Quality in Higher Education*. Phoenix, AZ: American Council on Education, Oryx Press, 1993.

Sims, S.J. *Student Outcomes Assessment: A Historical Review and Guide to Program Development*. New York: Greenwood Press, 1992.

Smith, P. *Killing the Spirit: Higher Education in America*. New York: Viking, 1990.

Southern Association of Colleges and Schools. *Criteria for Accreditation*. Atlanta, GA: Southern Association of Colleges and Schools, 1991.

Thompson, C.P., Alfred, R.L., and Lowther, M. "Institutional Effort: A Reality Based Model for Assessment of Community College Productivity." *Community College Review*, 1987, *15*, 28-37.

USA Today. "Tougher Oversight of Schools Needed" (editorial), August 1994, *123*.

Wingspread Group on Higher Education. *An American Imperative: Higher Expectations for Higher Education*. Racine, WI: Johnson Foundation, 1993.

Young, K.E. and Chambers, C.M. "Accrediting Agency Approaches to Academic Program Evaluation." In Craven, E.C. (ed.), *Academic Program Evaluation*. New Directions for Institutional Research No. 27. San Francisco: Jossey-Bass, 1980.

Chapter II

It is not sufficient to rest on the laurels of past success or the record of the present. For all its rich history, there are too many signs that higher education is not taking seriously its responsibility to maintain a strong commitment to undergraduate learning; to be accountable for products that are relevant, effective, and of demonstrable quality; and to provide society with the full benefits from investments in research and public service. Thus, the challenge to higher education is to be sufficiently responsive and adaptable in light of these new demands and to propel our nation to the forefront of a new era. Unless political leaders, educators, and the public accept this challenge, higher education soon may be a worn-out system that has seen its best days.

—Roy Romer, 1995
Governor of Colorado
Chairman, Education Commission of the States

Laurence F. Johnson
Associate Director
League for Innovation in the Community College
Mission Viejo, California

SURVEYING INSTITUTIONAL EFFECTIVENESS IN NORTH AMERICAN COMMUNITY COLLEGES

The underlying goal of any organization
is to improve effectiveness.
—P.T. Ewell and R.P. Lisensky, *Assessing Institutional Effectiveness*

More than a decade ago, ushered in by the publication of landmark reports such as *A Nation at Risk* (1983), *To Reclaim a Legacy* (1984), and *Involvement in Learning* (1984), a groundswell of activity arose as commissions, agencies, legislatures, and accrediting bodies moved educational effectiveness into the forefront of discussion. Virtually all of the regional accrediting associations, beginning with the Southern Association for Colleges and Schools in 1985, now have included provisions for demonstrating institutional effectiveness into their requirements for accreditation. *Campus Trends, 1990*, a survey by the American Council on Education, noted that 82 percent of all colleges were reporting some form of assessment activity, a huge jump from just 55 percent two years earlier (El-Khawas, 1990). Scores of articles and reports have been published on the topic.

What has been lacking in the rush of literature that has emerged over the past decade is a picture of how community colleges have embraced the institutional effectiveness movement and how and to what extent they are measuring their own performance. This study began with three major goals:

- To review important issues in the institutional effectiveness debate
- To describe the current extent of community colleges' adoption of institutional effectiveness measures and practices
- To identify and showcase selected community colleges that have been successful in comprehensively demonstrating institutional effectiveness.

The broad-brush views of the most common and controversial issues in the institutional effectiveness debate, touched upon in the opening chapter, will be explored further as we showcase college responses to institutional effectiveness concerns and issues in the remaining chapters. The current extent of community colleges' movements to demonstrate institutional effectiveness will be described here as we share the responses to our survey of North American community colleges. (See Appendix A for the full text of the survey.) Finally, we will end this discussion of survey responses by turning to the information we gathered through a final request of survey respondents—the information that became the primary focus of this investigation.

While we paid extraordinary attention to this final request for information from survey respondents, it is important first to describe the survey responses that make up our wide-angle perspective on the institutional effectiveness picture. These survey responses provide a current benchmark of college adoption of institutional effectiveness measurement tools and processes; more importantly, they paint the landscape upon which we have drawn portraits of institutional effectiveness particulars from selected community colleges.

What Is Institutional Effectiveness?

The first steps in developing and administering our survey of North American two-year colleges were to clarify the language in common use among practitioners and to clearly define what we meant by institutional effectiveness. We found a number of similar terms in the literature, including *outcomes assessment*, *outcomes measurement*, *institutional assessment*, and *institutional effectiveness*; but since 1985, when the Southern Association of Colleges and Schools (SACS) incorporated the systematic measurements of results into its accreditation procedures, the term *institutional effectiveness* has gradually come into broad usage. As Nichols (1991) notes, SACS chose this terminology consciously to distinguish the new focus embedded in its Criteria for Accreditation from "outcomes assessment," a phrase that had become unpalatable to many institutions because it had taken on a connotation of "measuring everything that moves" and was thought to imply a predominately departmental perspective. Nichols argues that "the term *institutional effectiveness* is more descriptive and inclusive of the identification of institutional and departmental programmatic intentions than is the term *outcomes assessment*" (p. 10). To be sure that we used language that conformed to current usage in community colleges, we included a question on appropriate terminology in our pilot survey of community college presidents. Along with what we saw as a gradual evolution in the terminology used in the literature, the responses to our pilot solidified our decision to use the term *institutional effectiveness*, but did not help a great deal in clarifying its meaning.

As we studied individual colleges and their definitions of institutional effectiveness, we realized that if we embraced all of the various nuances of their descriptions, our own would grow too complex, and, in fact, take us away from our goal of defining the landscape and showcasing successful programs. As the Community College Roundtable noted in its 1994 report, effectiveness eludes easy definition. The *Policy Statement on the Role and Value of Accreditation*, adopted in 1982 by the Council on Postsecondary Accreditation (COPA) provided an early and natural framework which set the tone of later efforts to define institutional effectiveness by declaring that an accredited institution "a) has appropriate purposes; b) has the resources to accomplish its purposes; c) can demonstrate that it is accomplishing its purposes"; [and] (d) gives reasons to believe that it will continue to accomplish its purposes" (no page number). The council clarified its thinking in its 1986 report, *Educational Quality and Accreditation*, which stated:

> The quality of an educational process relates to (1) the appropriateness of its objectives, (2) the effectiveness of the use of resources in pursuing these objectives, and (3) the degree to which objectives are achieved. Without a clear statement of what education is expected to provide, it is not possible to determine how good it is. (p. 4)

A number of writers have echoed these themes in their efforts to define institutional effectiveness. Grossman and Duncan describe it as "the process of articulating the mission of the college, setting goals, defining how the college and the community will know when these goals are being met, and using the data from assessment in an ongoing cycle of planning and evaluation" (1989, p. 5). Alfred and Kreider (1991) presented effectiveness as the ability of an institution to produce the outcomes it desires in the publics it serves. Ewell (1992) defined institutional effectiveness as the match between institutional purpose and performance. The Community College Roundtable suggested that an effective college "has a discernible mission, is producing outcomes that meet constituency needs, and can conclusively document the outcomes it is producing as a reflection of its mission" (1994, p. 8). Hudgins observed that, for most colleges, institutional effectiveness could be demonstrated by asking and answering three basic questions: What is the mission of the college? What are the major results expected from achieving the mission? What specific evidence will be accepted to show that these results have been achieved (1991)?

We resonated strongly to Edgerton's observation that the process of demonstrating institutional effectiveness "is a mindset that asks questions—good questions, hard questions, legitimate questions" (1990, p. 5). Our pilot study revealed that many believe institutional effectiveness flows strictly from the college's mission (or mission statement), but also that community colleges routinely track other measures that they consider very important in gauging overall effectiveness, but which are less easily traced to the formal mission statement. In order to capture the truest picture of what colleges actually consider to be measurements of effectiveness and to determine if colleges were basing their decisions on a firm theoretical framework or simply responding to pressure, we decided to take a very broad view that would allow us to cast a wide net. For the purposes of the survey, *institutional effectiveness activities were defined as any process by which any of several key indicators were measured routinely.*

What Should Community Colleges Be Measuring?

When we began assembling the information that would ultimately find its way into our survey, it quickly became apparent that there was no lack of models in the literature. A host of writers had outlined frameworks and measures for gauging institutional effectiveness for more than two decades (Community College Roundtable, 1994; Doucette and Hughes, 1990; Ewell, 1992; Nichols, 1991; and Roueche, Baker, and Brownell, 1972, to name but a few). The problem, rather, was in deciding which of the many frameworks available would be most applicable to community colleges and, thus, most appropriate as a foundation for our survey.

Much of the leading work in establishing models for institutional effectiveness can be traced to COPA's 1982 report. The Secretary of Education, William Bennett, expressed the essence of COPA's thinking and clarified it in 1985, when he indicated that "colleges should state their goals, measure their success in meeting those goals, and make the results available to everyone" ("Bennett Calls on Colleges...," 1985, p. 25). The National Alliance of Community and Technical Colleges' (NACTC) model of institutional effectiveness (Figure 1) formalizes this perspective (Grossman and Duncan, 1989).

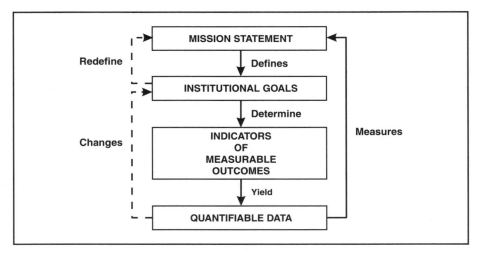

Figure 1: NACTC Model of Institutional Effectiveness

NACTC's model places the institutional mission statement at the top as the essential element from which goals and indicators flow. Key to the concept is the use of data from the measurement of indicators to assess and refine institutional goals. The process of goal-setting and evaluation may result in redefinition of the mission, most notably in cases where it is clear from the measurement process that a goal may be untenable.

Nichols used an adaptation of the rational planning model to conceptualize his view of institutional effectiveness for educational institutions, a model he calls the Institutional Effectiveness Paradigm (1991). In describing the paradigm, illustrated in Figure 2, he notes that it is a simple depiction of "activities that have been proposed, fostered, and occasionally practiced by many authors and institutions for a number of years" (Nichols, 1991, p. 12). The critical elements of Nichols' model amplify and expand earlier work:

- The establishment of an expanded statement of institutional purpose
- The identification of intended educational, research, service, and administrative objectives and outcomes
- The assessment of the extent to which the intended outcomes and objectives are being accomplished
- The adjustment of the institution's mission, objectives, outcomes, and activities based on the assessment findings.

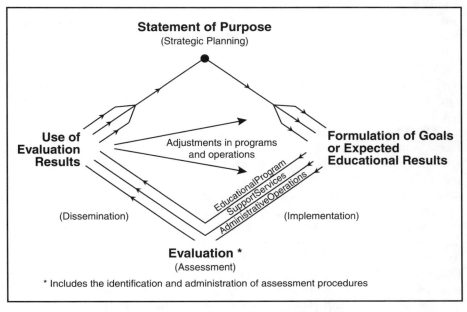

Figure 2: Components of a Planning and Evaluation Process

As Figure 2 details, Nichols' model emphasizes the importance of using evaluation results to effect improvements. Although Nichols' work did not flow from the total quality management (TQM) literature, TQM proponents will recognize many of the model's features. Nichols' Institutional Effectiveness Paradigm was ultimately incorporated into the Southern Association of Colleges and Schools' *Resource Manual on Institutional Effectiveness* (Commission on Colleges, 1989, p. 6).

Frameworks such as those provided by NACTC and Nichols have helped many colleges clarify their approach to designing their own models, but many continue to struggle with measurement issues. Spurred on by reports such as *A Nation at Risk, Time for Results,* and a good many others, federal agencies and state and provincial legislatures are defining objectives, outcomes, and measures for colleges. In 1990, Ewell, Finney, and Lenth found that 84 percent of state governing/coordinating boards either had identifiable assessment initiatives in place, or were planning immediate adoption of such initiatives—a substantial increase from the handful of states promoting assessment in 1985 (Hutchings and Marchese, 1990). As Boyer noted, "Governors and legislatures have placed the quality of undergraduate education squarely on the state agenda. The state boards aim to keep it there" (Boyer, Ewell, Finney, and Mingle, 1987, p. 11).

Our quest for relevant indicators to include in our survey led us to look closely at the kinds of measures states and provinces were requiring. We found many parallels, including requirements that colleges collect and submit data on student retention, graduation, transfer, and placement rates; minority enrollments and academic achievement; and the success of developmental students. Hudgins (1991, p. 3) suggests that colleges go further than required by the states, proposing that colleges also measure the success of transfer students at senior institutions, placement rates of graduates, satisfaction of employers, satisfaction of students with programs and services, and the impact of the institution on economic development.

Of all the sources of information on institutional effectiveness measures we found, however, none was as focused or conceptually coherent as the *Core Indicators of Effectiveness* compiled by the Community College Roundtable (1994). The roundtable, a special-purpose group of community college executive officers, university professors, and higher education officials, came together in December 1992 to address the need for "models to use in assessing effectiveness that are unique to the community college and that would reflect core measures implicit in its mission" (p. 4). Three organizations pooled people and resources to support the work of the group: the Community College Consortium, the Consortium for Institutional Effectiveness and Student Success in the Community College, and the Education Commission of the States.

The model developed by the roundtable, presented in Figure 3, combines 13 core indicators in seven critical areas into a conceptual framework that weaves both internal and external perspectives around the common theme of student progress. Core indicators, in this model, were defined as those that *must* be measured—as opposed to those that *should* be measured.

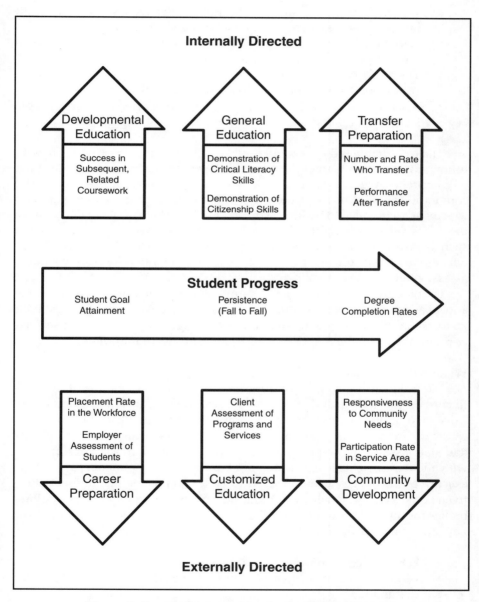

Figure 3: Core Indicators of Institutional Effectiveness

The reader will notice the explicit focus of the core indicators model on institutional mission. The roundtable detailed several significant benefits of this approach:

- The fundamental goal of institutional effectiveness—the desire to link purpose, resources, and outcomes is clear and explicit
- A foundation for understanding the interactive relationship between the college and the community is provided
- The breadth of community college activity is expressed and the strong correlation between organization and function is acknowledged
- A vast array of programs and tasks are categorized under a simple rubric (pp. 6-7).

The roundtable did not intend for these 13 indicators to provide an institution with a complete understanding of how the college was accomplishing its comprehensive mission, but rather with a sort of scorecard—"a few select core indicators that describe the major mission tasks that a community college must accomplish to be successful" (p. 6). The authors note that to achieve this focus, other important factors in institutional success have been omitted, such as institutional culture, strategic planning, resource allocation, and staff development. Nor did the authors intend the model to address substantive assessment of student learning.

Despite these limitations, the roundtable model offered considerable appeal as a structure for our study of the use of effectiveness indicators. With its focus on critical elements—the things a college *must* measure—it seemed appropriate to use the model as the basis for our list of indicators.

What Is the State of Current Practices?

We used several sources of information to assemble the list of 21 effectiveness indicators included in our survey. The work of the Community College Roundtable, described above, provided an initial list of 13 core indicators of effectiveness. A thorough review of the literature and of provincial and state assessment requirements provided other common indicators, and we validated their inclusion in the final survey with a pilot survey of chief executives in colleges acknowledged to be leaders in the institutional effectiveness movement. Finally, we contacted each of the six regional accrediting bodies for their accreditation criteria, which we used as additional sources of key indicators. We built the survey around six key questions/dimensions:

- What are community colleges measuring?
- What kinds of measures are required and by whom? What is under discussion?
- What groups are exerting the most influence on community colleges?

- Do community colleges know they are accomplishing their missions?
- What is the number one institutional effectiveness issue facing community colleges?
- What are the institutional demographics of the respondents?

Population

We chose to survey member colleges of the American Association of Community Colleges and Association of Canadian Community Colleges (AACC and ACCC). Initially, we planned to conduct a simple random survey of all member colleges, but a cursory study of the two groups' memberships showed that such a sample would likely increase the sampling error. Because a majority of members in both organizations are small colleges and technical schools, they would be overrepresented in the survey population, when the great majority of students attending North American community colleges are enrolled in large districts and colleges.

We chose, instead, a stratified random sampling procedure that would provide the benefits of randomness and allow for stratification along important population parameters (Kerlinger, 1986; Singleton, Straits, Straits, and McAllister, 1988). Member colleges of AACC and ACCC were divided into categories prior to our random selection of colleges within these categories. Because these categories were more homogeneous, they would reduce the sampling error that simple random sampling would create (Rubin and Babbie, 1993). Additionally, this stratification would facilitate more complete analyses of specific categories and comparisons between categories. The categories for this sample were:

- *Category One: Community College Districts or Systems*. Multicampus or multicollege organizations organized into districts or systems. (A notable exclusion from this stratum was the Community College of the Air Force. The data from this institution, which represents some 99 colleges and campuses, could have skewed the results for non-comparable institutions.)
- *Category Two: Large, Non-District-Affiliated Colleges*. Individual institutional members with 8,000 credit students or more, not associated with a district or system.
- *Category Three: Average, Non-District-Affiliated Colleges*. Individual institutional members, with less than 8,000 credit students, not affiliated with a district or system.

A random sample of 45 U.S. colleges and six Canadian colleges was drawn from each of these categories, generating a list of 147 institutions that spanned three-quarters of the states and four Canadian provinces; all six U.S. accrediting regions were represented. Our sampling plan facilitated comparisons between community college districts, large community colleges, and average community colleges.

While this was a small number of colleges in terms of the sample to population ratio for Category Three, we accepted the limitations of the smaller sample in order to keep it manageable. This was an important decision given the type of survey to be conducted. Our study sought data that may not be readily available, and so conducting a phone survey would be impractical. A mailed survey of selected colleges was the best available option. To avoid the problems typically associated with large-scale mail surveys (for example, low response rate, ranging from 30 to 40 percent), direct contact follow-up procedures were developed. These procedures, used in conjunction with a sample of manageable size, helped ensure a more representative sample.

We designed a survey instrument that would be appropriate for either a community college district (Category One) or a single community college (Categories Two and Three). Survey instruments were mailed to the CEO of each institution, or in the case of a district, to the district CEO only; a cover letter described the study and requested participation. Our letter requested data from fall 1995 and assured anonymity of individual responses, if requested. Non-respondents were contacted by phone and asked again to complete the survey.

Response Rates

The overall response rate to the survey was 61.2 percent. As illustrated in Figure 4, the responding institutions used in the analysis included colleges and districts from 34 states and three Canadian provinces, and the collected data represented the state-of-the-art of institutional effectiveness use in approximately eight percent of North American community colleges. Careful analysis of the surveys received revealed no systematic differences between the responding colleges and non-responding colleges in terms of geographic region, district size, or budget.

The response rate in this investigation is higher than that of typical national mail surveys. The sample represents approximately one-twelfth of the two-year colleges in North America. Additionally, many of the results reported here are very similar to other surveys reporting on institutional effectiveness (for example, Boyer et al., 1987; El-Khawas, 1990). Thus, even with the inevitable limitations, the data reported here can be regarded as effectively representing trends in institutional effectiveness in AACC and ACCC member colleges and, more specifically, within the stratified districts and colleges.

Institutional Demographics

As Table 1 illustrates, the respondents to our survey on North American colleges are generally representative of the broad landscape of institutions in the U.S. and Canada, except (as noted in the previous section) for the proportion of Category Three schools. Nonetheless, the respondents included a balanced mix of institutions in all of six demographic categories.

The majority of schools surveyed (67 percent) reported annual operating budgets of $20 million or more; 52 percent enrolled 10,000 or more credit students in the fall 1995 term. Responding colleges were roughly balanced in terms of location, with urban institutions representing 40 percent of respondents. Most (87 percent) were governed by a local board. Single-campus colleges accounted for slightly less than half (48 percent) of the respondents. The overwhelming majority described themselves as comprehensive community colleges, while technical colleges represented about eight percent of the respondents.

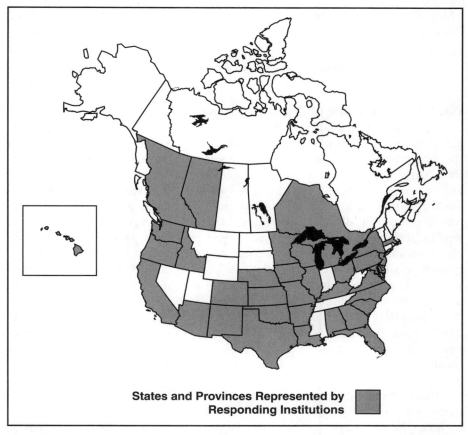

**States and Provinces Represented by
Responding Institutions**

Figure 4: States and Provinces Represented by Responding Institutions

Type of Institution		*Organization*	
Community college	90%	Single-campus college	48%
Technical college or institute	8%	College, multi-college district	25%
Junior college	2%	Multi-campus college	27%
Enrollment		*Budget*	
Less than 2,500	11%	Less than $ 5 million	3%
2,500 to 4,999	16%	$ 5 to 9.9 million	10%
5,000 to 9,999	23%	$ 10 to 19.9 million	19%
10,000 to 24,999	36%	$ 20 to 49.9 million	33%
More than 25,000	16%	More than $ 50 million	34%
Location		*Board of Trustees*	
Urban	40%	Elected local board	54%
Suburban	34%	Appointed local board	32%
Rural	26%	State/provincial board	14%

Table 1: Institutional Demographics of Respondents (n=90)

What Are Community Colleges Measuring?

As noted previously, we relied on several sources of information to assemble the list of 21 effectiveness indicators included in our survey, including the Community College Roundtable's core indicators of effectiveness. The literature, provincial and state assessment requirements, and the accrediting associations provided other common indicators that we used to round out our list, and our pilot survey of CEOs validated the inclusion of these indicators in our study. We asked respondents to tell us which of the 21 effectiveness indicators we finally assembled they were currently measuring. Colleges also were asked to rate each of the measures they were monitoring in terms of their relative importance, using a five-point scale which ranged from "not very important" to "critical." To ensure that we captured the kinds of indicators colleges were actually using, we also allowed respondents to provide us with other indicators and to rate their importance as well. Although some colleges added alternative indicators, none was echoed by even one other college, and no patterns or commonalities among these responses were discernible. The results, ranked by the proportion of colleges using each indicator, are presented in Table 2.

Community colleges continue to place a very high level of emphasis on traditional indicators. The two most common indicators—routinely tracked by more than 90 percent of colleges—were degree and certificate completion rates and growth. Also among the top five most commonly used indicators in our survey were cost containment, diversity, and the number and rate of students who transfer, all fairly traditional types of measures. (The appearance of cost containment near the top of the list is a reflection, no doubt, of the fiscal pressures that have troubled colleges in the last several years.) Despite the smaller proportion of colleges tracking mission-related indicators, the data show clearly that colleges are beginning to take a broader view of institutional assessment. Twenty of the 21 indicators we studied are tracked routinely by the majority of colleges.

Five of the seven categories of core indicators identified by the Community College Roundtable have found their way into broad use, and more than two-thirds of the colleges are monitoring these nine indicators. The roundtable's community development indicators were in use in approximately six of 10 colleges. Despite pressure from accrediting agencies and legislatures, the data show that colleges have been slow to adopt learning-relat-

Effectiveness Indicator	Percentage of Colleges Monitoring	Relative Importance of Indicator
Degree/Certificate Completion Rates	98%	4.2
Growth	94%	4.4
Cost Containment	89%	4.5
Promoting Diversity	89%	4.1
Number and Rate Who Transfer	89%	4.4
Persistence (Fall to Fall)	88%	4.3
Placement Rate in the Workforce	84%	4.5
Client Assessment of Programs and Services	80%	4.4
Faculty Productivity	79%	4.2
Student Goal Attainment	76%	4.5
Performance after Transfer	72%	4.5
Success in Subsequent, Related Coursework	71%	4.5
Employer Assessment of Students	68%	4.3
Faculty Satisfaction	66%	4.0
Participation Rate in Service Area	64%	4.1
Staff Satisfaction	63%	4.1
Responsiveness to Community Needs	58%	4.3
Staff Productivity	58%	4.2
Use of Indicators/Measures for Planning	58%	4.4
Demonstration of Critical Literacy Skills	52%	4.3
Demonstration of Citizenship Skills	20%	3.4

Table 2: Usage and Perceived Importance of Common Indicators

ed indicators. One of the general education indicators suggested by the roundtable (demonstration of critical literacy skills) was ranked second to last on our list, while the other, demonstration of citizenship skills, was at the bottom, currently measured by only 20 percent of respondents.

Chi-square analyses were conducted on the respondents' ratings of each indicator's relative importance using the demographic categories presented in Table 1. No significant differences were found in the ratings of any indicator's importance when grouped by region, type of institution, organization, or enrollment. Significant relationships ($p<.05$) were found, however, between the type of board and the importance assigned to several indicators. Colleges with local elected boards were found to rate growth, student transfer, and community responsiveness indicators higher in importance than did colleges with appointed or state boards. Colleges with budgets under $10 million tended to rate growth as more important than did other colleges ($p< .05$), no doubt a reflection of the impact of growth-driven funding formulas and the relatively greater importance of state and provincial funding to smaller institutions. Rural schools tended to place more importance on monitoring critical literacy skills than did colleges in either urban or suburban locales ($p <.05$).

Canadian and U.S. colleges were in remarkable agreement on the importance of most indicators, although Canadian colleges rated growth and staff satisfaction as more important on average than did U.S. colleges ($p<.05$). One factor that should be considered in interpreting the difference in importance of staff satisfaction between the two countries is that all of the responding Canadian colleges monitored staff satisfaction, in contrast to 63 percent of U.S. colleges.

What Kinds of Measures Are Required and By Whom?
What Is Under Discussion?

Our survey asked colleges to indicate which of the Community College Roundtable's core indicators they were required to monitor by their boards of trustees, funding agencies, or accrediting bodies. A mechanism was included to allow colleges to list other indicators they might be monitoring or other groups that may be requiring certain indicators. The responses to these open-ended items indicate that internal processes at many colleges are imposing requirements beyond those expected by trustees, funding agencies, or the accrediting associations. While these internal pressures affect only a small proportion of colleges (responses indicating some form of internal requirements ranged from 11 to 21 percent across all the indicators), they also indicate that a significant proportion of colleges are taking more control and interest in the kinds of data that can confirm the effectiveness of their efforts.

Internal groups are most likely to require data on client assessments of programs and services, a reflection of the customer focus that many colleges have adopted. Internal groups in about one-fifth of colleges are asking important questions about developmental programs, particularly how these students are doing in subsequent, related coursework. Other self-imposed indicators found in approximately 20 percent of responding colleges are data on degree/completion rates, transfer data (including student performance after transfer), and workforce placement rates.

The most common core indicators required of colleges by external groups are degree/completion and workforce placement rates, with pressure for these measures coming from all directions—funding agencies, accrediting bodies, boards, and internal constituencies. Funding agencies and the regional associations are increasingly requiring colleges to provide data on the number and rate of students who transfer, client assessment of programs and services, and the success of developmental students in subsequent, related coursework.

Student performance after transfer is noted by colleges to be an emerging issue of concern to accrediting bodies, a finding borne out by the fact that the indicator is listed as an example of one way to measure student achievement in publications by SACS (Commission on Colleges, 1989, p. 10) and the Middle States Association (Commission on Higher Education, 1991, p. 36). The North Central Association, which has made assessment of student academic achievement a priority, also lists measures of this type (Lopez, 1996), but notes that these should be considered as *indirect* measures of student learning. What is apparent from the responses to our survey is that student academic assessment is a major issue for colleges in the North Central region; however, in most areas of North America, learning-related measures are more likely to be topics of discussion than requirements, partly because of the difficulty both colleges and accrediting bodies are having in defining appropriate measures.

What Groups Are Exerting the Most Pressure on Community Colleges?

We asked colleges to rate the top three sources of influence on their adoption of effectiveness measures and practices. Our list of possible influences included boards of trustees, legislatures, regulatory agencies, federal agencies, regional and programmatic accrediting bodies, and collective bargaining processes. To ensure that no significant sources of influence were omitted, we provided an open-ended item. About 17 percent of colleges chose that item to indicate that internal groups or processes were an important influence on their institutional effectiveness practices.

Clearly, the most significant pressure on colleges to move to more comprehensive assessment is coming from the regional accrediting bodies. The accrediting bodies were ranked among the top three influences on college institutional effectiveness practices by 76 percent of responding colleges. This finding is not surprising, as the regional associations, particularly the

Southern and North Central Associations, have provided considerable leadership to colleges beginning to venture into assessment policies and practices. Institutional effectiveness has become a central component of the accreditation review process in all six regions. Other highly significant influences were the institution's board of trustees, ranked in the top three by 57 percent of colleges, and state or provincial legislators, ranked in the top three by 50 percent of respondents.

Collective bargaining agreements were listed as key influences by about eight percent of colleges. To help understand and interpret the role of collective bargaining processes, several colleges were contacted for additional information. For some colleges, movement toward increased measurement of effectiveness has been hampered by strong employee resistance; unfortunately for these institutions, the measurement or use of some types of indicators (staff productivity or faculty satisfaction, for example) has been prohibited by collective bargaining agreements.

Do Community Colleges Know They Are Accomplishing Their Missions?

We asked colleges to tell us if they had a formal, board-approved mission statement, if their mission statement included explicit objectives, and if those objectives were routinely monitored. Despite the overwhelming theme in the institutional effectiveness literature of the importance of measurable objectives being tied to the institution's mission statement, the data show clearly that most colleges are not collecting the kinds of information that would tell them whether they are accomplishing their missions. While all responding colleges reported having a formal mission statement, only 64 percent had linked measurable objectives to the mission, and barely one-third of colleges were routinely measuring mission-linked objectives.

As Table 3 details, considerable variation in practice was found by region; all responding colleges in the Northwest region had mission-linked objectives, with 80 percent reporting that these objectives were routinely measured. Most U.S. colleges fell far short of that level of implementation. About six in 10 U.S. colleges reported having formal mission-related objectives, yet barely half of those institutions were monitoring such objectives. The situation was worse in Canada. Only about 43 percent of Canadian colleges linked objectives to mission, and only a scant 18 percent were monitoring those objectives.

Notably, as Table 4 illustrates, a pattern emerged related to institutional size; having formal mission-related objectives was most common in smaller schools of less than 5,000 students. The presence and follow-up of these kinds of objectives were least likely in very large colleges with enrollments of more than 25,000 students.

This finding was echoed when colleges were classified according to budget categories, as Table 5 illustrates. Less than half of colleges with budgets

Region	Formal Objectives Linked to Mission Statement	Mission-Related Objectives Routinely Monitored
Northwest	100%	80%
Southern	65%	36%
North Central	63%	37%
Western	60%	27%
Middle States	60%	24%
Canada	43%	18%
Average	**64%**	**34%**

Note: The New England area had too few cases to classify.

**Table 3: Percentage of Sampled Colleges Linking and
Monitoring Mission-Related Objectives by Region**

greater than $50 million had formal objectives linked to their mission statements, and only 21 percent monitored such objectives. Although the number of schools with very small budgets (under $5 million) was small, all of these institutions routinely monitored mission-linked objectives.

What Is the Number One Issue?

Our pilot survey asked CEOs to identify key unresolved issues in the institutional effectiveness debate; we used the issues they identified to ask all surveyed colleges what they considered to be the number one issue facing two-year colleges. Included in our list were the selection and design of appro-

Enrollment	Formal Objectives Linked to Mission Statement	Mission-Related Objectives Routinely Monitored
More than 25,000	38%	17%
10,000 to 24,999	64%	34%
5,000 to 9,999	60%	30%
2,500 to 4,999	86%	49%
Less than 2,500	70%	42%

**Table 4: Percentage of Sampled Colleges Linking and Monitoring
Mission-Related Objectives by Enrollment (Fall 1995)**

Operating Budget	Formal Objectives Linked to Mission Statement	Mission-Related Objectives Routinely Monitored
More than $50 million	48%	21%
$20 to 49.9 million	66%	41%
$10 to 19.9 million	76%	31%
$5 to 9.9 million	67%	38%
Less than $5 million	100%	100%

Table 5: Percentage of Sampled Colleges Linking and Monitoring Mission-Related Objectives by Operating Budget (1995-96 fiscal year)

priate measures, the measurement of student learning, staff commitment and willingness to evaluate college practices, and outcomes-based funding. As we did with other parts of the survey, an open-ended item was included to allow colleges to suggest issues not on our list.

The data on this item indicate that many colleges are encountering considerable challenges in creating an institutional climate conducive to ongoing measurement of effectiveness. The number-one-rated issue related to institutional effectiveness for community colleges was staff commitment and willingness to evaluate college practices, listed by 36 percent of respondents. Other key issues of concern indicate that colleges are uncertain how to best measure some outcomes. About one in four colleges listed measurement-related issues as key challenges, including how to select and design appropriate measures and how to appropriately measure student learning.

Summary of Findings

Overall, our survey confirmed that North American community colleges are taking significant steps to demonstrate their effectiveness—albeit slowly, given the tremendous body of work in institutional effectiveness that has accumulated over the last decade. While most of the impetus towards better and more effective assessment is being imposed on colleges from without, nearly one in five colleges are embracing the concept and adopting practices that exceed those required by their boards or external groups.

At the same time, given the fact that the overwhelming majority of colleges are not engaged in the kinds of data collection activities that would tell them if, in fact, their missions are being accomplished, it appears that the conceptual frameworks advanced in the literature—most of which center on the connection between mission and expected outcomes—have not been adopted on any large scale. Colleges, for the most part, do not appear to understand the link between institutional mission and effectiveness. The other key findings of this survey can be summarized as follows:

- Community colleges continue to place a very high level of emphasis on traditional indicators. Nonetheless, colleges are beginning to take a broader view of institutional assessment—20 of the 21 indicators we studied are routinely tracked by a majority of colleges. The five most commonly used indicators in our survey were degree and completion rates, growth, cost containment, diversity, and the number and rate of students who transfer. Despite pressure from accrediting agencies and legislatures, colleges have been slow to adopt learning-related indicators; the two core general education indicators suggested by the Community College Roundtable ranked at the bottom of our list, with students' citizenship skills being measured by only 20 percent of respondents.

- The most common core indicators required of colleges are degree/completion and workforce placement rates, with pressure for these measures coming from all directions—funding agencies, accrediting bodies, boards, and internal constituencies. Funding agencies and the regional associations are increasingly requiring colleges to provide data on the number and rate of students who transfer, client assessment of programs and services, and the success of developmental students in subsequent, related coursework. Student performance after transfer is an emerging issue of concern to both accrediting bodies and internal college groups. Assessment of student academic achievement is a major issue for colleges in the North Central region; but otherwise, learning-related measures are more likely to be topics of discussion than requirements.

- Clearly, the most significant pressure on colleges to move to more comprehensive assessment is coming from the regional accrediting bodies. The regional associations, particularly the Southern and North Central Associations, have provided considerable leadership to colleges as institutional effectiveness and the assessment of student achievement have become central components of the accreditation review process in all six regions. The accrediting bodies were ranked among the top three influences on college institutional effectiveness practices by 76 percent of responding colleges. Other significant influences were the institution's board of trustees, ranked in the top three by 57 percent of the colleges, and state or provincial legislators, ranked in the top three by 50 percent of the respondents.

- Despite the overwhelming theme in the institutional effectiveness literature of the importance of measurable objectives being tied to the
  institution's mission statement, colleges generally are not collecting
  the kinds of information that would tell them whether they are
  accomplishing their missions. While all responding colleges reported
  having a formal mission statement, only 64 percent had linked measurable objectives to the mission, and barely one-third of colleges
  were routinely measuring mission-linked objectives. Considerable
  variation in practice was found by region; all responding colleges in
  the Northwest region had mission-linked objectives, with 80 percent
  reporting that these objectives were routinely measured. Just 43 percent of Canadian colleges linked objectives to mission, and only a
  scant 18 percent were monitoring those objectives. Notably, a pattern
  emerged related to institutional size; these kinds of practices were
  found to be least likely in very large colleges with enrollments of
  more than 25,000 students and budgets greater than $50 million, and
  were relatively more common among smaller institutions.
- Colleges are encountering considerable challenges in creating an
  institutional climate conducive to ongoing measurement of effectiveness. The number-one-rated issue related to institutional effectiveness for community colleges was staff commitment and willingness
  to evaluate college practices, listed by 36 percent of the respondents.
  Other key issues of concern are how to select and design appropriate
  measures, and how student learning should be most appropriately
  measured.

The Results of Referential Sampling

Of the three goals we identified early on, we believed that showcasing
successful institutional effectiveness programs was the most critical. We had
determined that, by far, it was the most useful of all the information we were
gathering. In truth, we did not expect much to have changed during the
dozen years that had passed since *A Nation at Risk* captured the attention of
policymakers across the continent. While evidence of the increasing interest
in institutional effectiveness abounds in the literature, the wide variety of
commentaries, descriptions, and studies have resulted in little more than a
continuing affirmation of the notion that measurement of effectiveness is a
concept being imposed on colleges from without. The general literature has
not produced any evidence of national trends; no trends have emerged from
these studies that indicate how best to set about measuring institutional effectiveness. It was apparent that the next step in the study of North American
institutional effectiveness practices must be to identify and study significant
community college programs and systems that appear to be working, to
detail the most common characteristics of their successes, and to use them to

craft broad-brush recommendations for institutional policy design and implementation.

Therefore, as the final request of our pilot survey respondents, we asked for help in locating districts and colleges that have exceptional programs and policies for effectively utilizing institutional effectiveness. They were encouraged to identify themselves if they believed their own programs and policies were effective. We asked for the names of institutions and appropriate contacts at each. As we contacted the individuals and institutions identified in our survey, we asked for further information about other exceptional programs. This referential sampling procedure provided us with the names of the authors and colleges that are featured in the following chapters.

As we assembled the list of college presidents to be invited to submit chapters, we did not wish to adopt a purely "best practices" approach. Rather, as noted in the introduction to this chapter, our intention was to paint the broad landscape of college responses to the push for demonstrated institutional effectiveness. We felt it important, therefore, to include a mix of colleges—large and small, urban and rural, and those with well-established and less-well-established institutional effectiveness models. The following chapters include colleges that have been fine-tuning their assessment practices for many years and have built considerable acceptance for and commitment to measuring and evaluating college practices within their institutions. We also have included colleges that have not traveled very far and asked them to describe the challenges they face daily as they strive to create a climate conducive to ongoing measurement.

In each case, the colleges featured in following chapters have important stories to tell. Some, written with the clarity of 20/20 hindsight, offer suggestions and insight into the avoidable pitfalls. Others offer considerable detail on process and on how to involve the many college constituencies in meaningful ways. Most importantly, all add substance to the findings of our national survey by detailing how the results of measurement activities have been used in practice to inform planning and budget processes.

Conclusions

In large part, the findings from this national survey replicate and extend prior research in the area of institutional effectiveness, providing a wide-angle picture of the status of two-year colleges in North America. Judging from these data, it is apparent that institutional effectiveness is gradually taking hold in North American community colleges, driven largely by pressure from funding agencies, the regional accrediting associations (notably the Southern and North Central Associations of Colleges and Schools), and colleges' own boards of trustees.

The wide-angle picture detailed in this chapter provides a useful and informative context for assessing the progress of the institutional effectiveness movement, but our attention must turn now to a more focused look at what individual colleges are doing and how they have come to this point. In the chapters that follow, we move to an exploration of strategies in current use among representative colleges that have produced documented successes. In our final chapter, this wide-angle view will be revisited and set as the backdrop for a look to the future of the effectiveness movement.

REFERENCES

Alfred, R. and Kreider, P. "Creating a Culture for Institutional Effectiveness." *Community, Technical, and Junior College Journal*, 1991, *61*(5), 34-40.

"Bennett Calls on Colleges to Assess Their Own Performance, Publish Results." *Chronicle of Higher Education*, November 6, 1985, 25.

Boyer, C., Ewell, P., Finney, J., and Mingle, J. "Assessment and Outcomes Measurement: A View from the States." *AAHE Bulletin*, 1987, *39*(7), 8-12.

Commission on Colleges. *Resource Manual on Institutional Effectiveness.* Decatur, GA: Southern Association of Colleges and Schools, 1989.

Commission on Higher Education. *Designs for Excellence: Handbook for Institutional Self-Study.* Philadelphia: Middle States Association of Colleges and Schools, 1991.

Community College Roundtable. *Community Colleges: Core Indicators of Effectiveness.* Washington, DC: American Association of Community Colleges, 1994.

Council on Postsecondary Accreditation (COPA). *Policy Statement on the Role and Value of Accreditation.* Washington, DC: Council on Postsecondary Accreditation, 1982.

Council on Postsecondary Accreditation (COPA). *Educational Quality and Accreditation: A Call for Diversity, Continuity, and Innovation.* Washington, DC: Council on Postsecondary Accreditation, 1986.

Doucette, D. and Hughes, B. *Assessing Institutional Effectiveness in Community Colleges.* Laguna Hills, CA: League for Innovation in the Community College, 1990.

Edgerton, R. "Assessment at Half Time." *Change*, October 1990, *22*(5), 4-5.

El-Khawas, E. *Campus Trends, 1990.* (Higher Education Panel Report, No. 80). Washington, DC: American Council on Education, 1990.

Ewell, P.T. *Outcomes Assessment, Institutional Effectiveness, and Accreditation.* Resource Papers for the Council on Postsecondary Accreditation Task Force on Institutional Effectiveness, 1992. (ERIC Document Reproduction Service No. 343 513).

Ewell, P.T., Finney, J., and Lenth, C. "Filling in the Mosaic: The Emerging Pattern of State-Based Assessment." *AAHE Bulletin*, 1990, *42* (8), 3-5.

Ewell, P.T. and Lisensky, R.P. *Assessing Institutional Effectiveness: Redirecting the Self-Study Process.* Balden, CO: Consortium for the Advancement of Private Higher Education, 1991, p. 19.

Grossman, G.M. and Duncan, M.E. *Indications of Institutional Effectiveness: A Process for Assessing Two-Year Colleges.* Columbus, OH: Center on Education and Training for Employment, 1989.

Hudgins, J. "Institutional Effectiveness: A Strategy for Institutional Renewal." *Southern Association of Community, Junior, and Technical Colleges Occasional Paper*, 1991, *9* (1), 1-4.

Hutchings, P. and Marchese, T. "Watching Assessment: Questions, Stories, Prospects." *Change*, October 1990, 22(5), 12-38.

Kerlinger, F.N. *Foundations of Behavioral Research.* 3rd ed. Chicago: Holt, Rinehart, and Winston, 1986.

Lopez, C.L. "Opportunities for Improvement: Advice from Consultant-Evaluators on Programs to Assess Student Learning." Staff Paper, North Central Accreditation Commission on Institutions of Higher Education, March 1996.

Nichols, J.O. *A Practitioner's Handbook for Institutional Effectiveness and Student Outcomes Assessment Implementation.* New York: Agathon Press, 1991.

Roueche, J.E., Baker, G.A., III, and Brownell, R.L. *Accountability and the Community College: Directions for the 70's.* Washington, DC: American Association of Community and Junior Colleges, 1972.

Rubin, A. and Babbie, E. *Research Methods for Social Work.* 2nd ed. Pacific Grove, CA: Brooks/Cole, 1993.

Singleton, R., Jr., Straits, B.C., Straits, M.M., and MacAllister, R.J. *Approaches to Social Research.* New York: Oxford University Press, 1988.

Chapter III

Jim Hudgins, president, and Starnell Williams, vice president for advancement, at Midlands Technical College (SC), describe the current paradigm shift in the public's thinking about higher education, the challenges that this new thinking has created, and the accomplishments that are possible for colleges that choose to address current effectiveness challenges as opportunities.

They review Midlands' extensive experience with the institutional effectiveness movement, beginning with the college's reaffirmation of accreditation using the Southern Association of Colleges and Schools' (SACS) Criteria *that focused on outcome measures. The result of this experience is a comprehensive planning and evaluation system utilizing data to improve administrative and teaching processes. The chapter embraces Peter Ewell's charge: "the essential future task for self-regulation is to help render what we actually do in our institutions consistent with what we historically have said we believed in."[1]*

Three-year strategic planning cycles and annual action strategies—developed from priority initiatives—put theory into practice at Midlands Tech. An annual planning calendar outlines major planning and data-collection activities, assists in monitoring progress, and expedites appropriate responses to unexpected developments throughout the academic year. Three overarching questions about mission, results, and evidence produced six critical success factors, 19 indicators of effectiveness, and appropriate standards (benchmarks) by which to judge success. The Report Card, *a yearly update on the effectiveness program, shares the most recent data on collegewide assessment activities and effectiveness standards; and provides critical data for the external annual update,* Community Report, *that is mailed to more than 5,000 members of the community. This chapter describes several current activities that illustrate Midlands' use of institutional effectiveness data to measure college success with client satisfaction, institutional climate, and student learning. It outlines a reasonable, practical approach to fulfill requirements of external agencies and to establish a structure for institutional renewal.*

---

[1]Ewell, P.T. "A Matter of Integrity: Accountability and the Future of Self-Regulation." *Change*, November/December, 1994, 26, 24-29.

James L. Hudgins, *President*
Starnell K. Williams, *Vice President for Advancement*
Midlands Technical College
Columbia, South Carolina

SEIZING THE OPPORTUNITY OF
INSTITUTIONAL EFFECTIVENESS

*In my professional lifetime, few issues have vexed the
academic world so deeply as accountability has today.*
—T. Marchese

The mid-1980s marked a paradigm shift in the way business leaders and elected officials think about and deal with higher education. This new way of viewing higher education goes by a variety of titles: government officials call it *accountability*; accrediting officials call it *institutional effectiveness*; faculty members call it *assessment*; and, unfortunately, too many faculty and administrators call it a *fad*.

Whatever it is called, this new approach to evaluating the role of education in American society has taken on the characteristics of a movement:

- More than 40 states have accountability mandates.
- Many states have incorporated outcomes data into funding formulas.
- All six regional accrediting bodies focus on outcomes.
- The federal government has passed student right-to-know legislation.
- Business leaders who have reorganized and restructured their workplaces are calling for a similar response from higher education.

In short, everyone seems to be asking college leaders, "What and how much are your students learning?" For community colleges, all this attention to institutional effectiveness and accountability presents an unparalleled opportunity—and we should gladly meet the task.

From their inception, community colleges have been results-oriented. We have, as a movement, measured our progress in terms of student success and community impact. Before it was fashionable or required, community colleges regularly reported placement data, licensure exam scores, retention rates, transfer success, and economic impact. Therefore, it is not surprising that Peter Ewell (1994) and other researchers of accountability issues report that community colleges are more responsive than senior colleges to accountability mandates.

Institutional effectiveness offers to community colleges our greatest opportunity in 100 years to be understood and valued for our contribution to our community and nation, and to be measured by our own standards. For most of our history, we have been compared to and measured by four-year college standards—and have not measured up. It is not that the standards were too high, but rather that they were the wrong standards. We must not miss this opportunity to establish a new paradigm for evaluating community colleges. Today's challenge is to seize the opportunity of institutional effectiveness and in doing so to accomplish three things:

- To do the right thing
- To demonstrate value
- To improve teaching and learning.

The Opportunity to Do the Right Thing

Since higher education is about teaching and learning, about preparing for life, and about influencing values, we should expect to be held accountable. The surprise should be over higher education's resistance to the accountability movement. The president of a major land grant university was describing the resistance of his faculty to the restructuring of the university. He noted that one would expect well-educated faculty, who purport to be on the cutting edge of knowledge, to be the leaders of the movement. Unfortunately, at his university they were leading the resistance.

However, an American public that invests more than $400 billion a year on education has a right to call for a report card, and the winds of change are blowing toward colleges and universities answering accountability questions from students, parents, taxpayers, policymakers, and legislators. A major response to the increasing national interest in reporting procedures and effectiveness data is the technical conventions manual, released in 1996 by the Joint Commission on Accountability Reporting (JCAR)—a commission created by the American Association of Community Colleges (AACC), American Association of State Colleges and Universities (AASCU), and National Association of State Universities and Land-Grant Universities (NAULGU). This manual offers colleges and universities important guidelines by which they can answer effectively the most common accountability questions. National discussions have indicated that accountability reporting is the right thing to do, that higher education's credibility with the public is suffering from a paucity of understandable, straightforward, and comparable information. The overarching question can no longer be: "Should we be account-able?" Rather, it must be: "How shall we demonstrate accountability?"

The Opportunity to Demonstrate Value

As previously noted, community colleges have lived in the shadow of research universities. We have been criticized in several national studies for not living up to four-year college standards. The accountability movement provides an opportunity for community colleges to define our mission and expected outcomes for the public.

However, recent research suggests that the mission of the community college correlates with the current needs and priorities of our nation. Harvey and Immerwahr (1995) conducted a major study for the American Council on Education to evaluate the public perception of higher education. They analyzed all the public surveys of higher education between 1989 and 1992 and organized focus groups in the four quadrants of the country to affirm the accuracy of their findings. They found that (1) the general public believes that the purpose of a college education is to acquire a credential for employment, and (2) community and business leaders—at least those surveyed by Harvey and Immerwahr—believe that the principal role of colleges and universities is to prepare a highly educated workforce. Both perceptions match the mission of the community college. As taxpayers and elected officials talk about "return on investment" and appeal to public agencies to offer cost-effective solutions to the challenges facing our nation, community college leaders are offered their greatest opportunity to promote the relevance and responsiveness of our institutions.

The Opportunity to Improve Teaching and Learning

By asking good, hard questions about what our students are learning, community colleges are improving the teaching and learning process. Someone once quipped: "You're doing good—that's good. You're doing bad—that's good. You don't know—that's bad."

It is no longer acceptable for a college to say we do not know or cannot measure the outcomes of education. While complex and difficult, we must make the effort. Therefore, Midlands Technical College (MTC) has made a sincere effort to define and measure the impact of our college on our students and community. We are not perfect, but we are persistent. The principal purpose of this chapter is to illustrate how we use institutional effectiveness to improve the teaching and learning process.

Midlands Technical College was fortunate to get in on the ground floor of the institutional effectiveness movement in the mid-1980s when the Southern Association of Colleges and Schools (SACS) moved from process- to outcomes-oriented accreditation. Perceiving the growing movement toward outcomes assessment, MTC volunteered to pursue reaffirmation of accreditation in 1987 using the new *Criteria for Accreditation* (SACS, 1991) that focused on outcome measures. We developed a comprehensive planning and evaluation system that was adopted as the core management strategy for our college.

We asked three questions:

- What is the mission of our college?
- What are the major results we expect from the achievement of our mission?
- What specific evidence are we willing to accept that these results have been achieved?

We have answered those questions by agreeing on six factors critical to the success of our college and 19 indicators (measures) of effectiveness for which we developed standards (benchmarks). As we have used the data collected in the process to plan and make decisions, we have been guided by the advice of Philip Crosby of the total quality management movement: "It is not what you find, but what you do with what you find" (1979, p. 65).

We have used the data we found to celebrate success and to improve deficiencies. Fortunately, most community colleges find that the measurement of outcomes provides multiple opportunities to recognize and reward faculty and staff for their accomplishments. The real test of an effectiveness program, however, is the willingness and ability of an institution to utilize data to improve the administrative and teaching processes at the college.

Laying the Foundation for the Effectiveness Process

Consensus within the college is critical to developing the foundation elements of vision, values, mission, role and scope, and goals. Whatever the process, the foundation on which the strategic plan is based must be fully understood and supported by the entire college. A clear understanding of the vision and mission is essential before operational tasks can be accomplished effectively. Although a number of processes are available to lead a college through the development of foundation elements, no single way can be cited as best. The assurances of belonging and participation are more critical than the methodology.

The foundation elements that began in conjunction with MTC's reaffirmation process are now reviewed during the three-year strategic planning cycle. The foundation elements—vision, values, mission, role and scope, and goals—were subjected to intensive scrutiny by a broad spectrum of the college community. The process used to develop the statements consisted of an ongoing discussion throughout the college community related to the philosophical role of the college—for example, who we are, who we should become, and how we should proceed to reach this desired state.

The college used several mechanisms to encourage the open exchange of ideas for the appropriate wording for the foundation elements. Mechanisms included survey questionnaires, focus groups, and a series of task forces. Surveys and focus group discussions were conducted with numerous college constituencies where input was solicited about the college's mission, its current level of performance, and satisfaction with the programs and services currently offered. The results from these sessions were used in the reports prepared by the task forces. Initial drafts of the foundation elements were prepared by the task forces and submitted for review by senior administrators. Each task force was comprised of senior administrators, midlevel managers, staff members, and students. The MTC Board of Trustees was fully informed of the progress made on developing these statements. In each iteration, the Executive Council reviewed and edited documents, and returned them to the college community for additional discussion and input. This process continued until all groups were satisfied with the results.

The college executive team then drafted the long-range goals and priority initiatives, and again the documents were shared with various college constituencies until consensus was reached. The foundation statements, institutional goals, and priority initiatives were compiled to form the institution's strategic plan. The *Strategic Plan* is published and widely shared with the college's internal and external community. All elements of this document remain unchanged for the entire period of the strategic planning cycle, and annual action strategies are developed from the priority initiatives.

Putting Theory into Practice

Operational planning, an ongoing process at MTC, provides the details for translating the college's priority initiatives into action. Each spring, each department and unit of the college develops a set of annual action strategies for the next fiscal year, beginning on July 1. The department's or unit's objectives and action plans are reviewed by the appropriate vice president or director to ensure that they correlate well with the college's goals and priority initiatives.

Through a process involving all stakeholders of the college, action strategies are identified that will move the college toward attaining its priority initiatives. At MTC, this process leads to the development of an annual budget and the allocation of resources. The commitment of college resources in support of the strategic plan is a significant factor in conveying to the college community that the board of trustees and the president are committed to institutional effectiveness.

To facilitate the assessment work that must be accomplished during a given year, MTC annually prepares and distributes an *Assessment Activities Plan*. This plan identifies collegewide action strategies, outlines the dates when major planning and assessment activities will occur, lists the standards for the indicators of effectiveness, and delineates the externally mandated assessment reports that must be completed during the year.

The document is compiled in the following way. Each action strategies form is used by the college's divisions to submit their annual action strategies to the office of Assessment, Research, and Planning (ARP). Action strategies must be related to the college's priority initiatives. Gaining additional input from each unit of the college through leadership organizations, such as the staff and faculty councils, the office of ARP then compiles the suggested work activities into a list of annual action strategies.

The office of ARP also drafts an annual planning calendar that outlines the major planning and data collection activities for the college. The Executive Council has established a series of planning dates that are devoted to establishing the annual operational plan for the next year, reviewing the results of the previous action strategies, and making midyear adjustments to activities and resource allocations based on realities that may occur unexpectedly during the year. Submission dates for reporting on the annual action strategies and providing mandated assessment reports are included on the calendar.

A draft document is then reviewed and finalized by the Executive Council and distributed to all appropriate members of the college community. The *Assessment Activities Plan* outlines the majority of collegewide assessment activities and is a road map for the completion of yearlong responsibilities.

Evaluation of Results: Matching Performance to Purpose

Distinct from traditional strategic or operational planning, institutional effectiveness requires a comprehensive evaluation system that measures the results of the college's programs and services. While strategic planning produces an operational blueprint, institutional effectiveness fundamentally relies on an outcomes-based assessment of actual achievement compared to intended results. In order to determine if performance matches purpose, MTC uses a set of benchmarks known as critical success factors. These factors must be successfully implemented for an organization to flourish and achieve its goals (Bullen and Rockart, 1981).

Given the magnitude and complexity of all that colleges do, it is valuable to limit evaluation to the most important areas. At MTC, a modified Delphi process was used initially to establish the most important benchmarks that would ensure the institution's success. Six critical success factors were identified which, if achieved, would be accepted by the college as positive proof of its effectiveness:

- Accessible, comprehensive programs of high quality
- Student satisfaction and retention

- Post-education satisfaction and success
- Economic development and community involvement
- Sound, effective resource management
- Dynamic organizational involvement and development.

To monitor and measure how well the college is performing relative to each critical success factor, MTC established indicators of effectiveness. These

-A- Accessible, Comprehensive Programs of High Quality	A-1 Access and Equity	A-2 Achievement in General Education	A-3 Assessment of the Academic Major	A-4 Successful Articulation/ Transfer
-B- Student Satisfaction and Retention	B-1 Accurate Entry Testing and Course Placement	B-2 Retention to Achievement of Student Goals	B-3 Student Satisfaction	B-4 Assessment of Student Services
-C- Post-Education Satisfaction and Success	C-1 Graduate Employment/ Continuing Education	C-2 Employer Satisfaction with Graduates	C-3 Alumni Satisfaction and Support	
-D- Economic Development and Community Involvement	D-1 Education in Support of Economic Development	D-2 Positive Community/ College Interaction		
-E- Sound, Effective Resource Management	E-1 Acquisition of Public/Private Resources	E-2 Facility Adequacy, Use and Condition	E-3 Distribution of Resources	
-F- Dynamic Organizational Involvement and Development	F-1 Ongoing Professional Development of Commission, Faculty and Staff	F-2 Affirmative Action Plan	F-3 Support for Equity in Employee Salary/Benefits	

**Table 1: MTC Critical Success Factors and
Institutional Effectiveness Indicators**

indicators, identified as the most important expected outcomes, represent a comprehensive evaluation of the college's programs and services. To determine the appropriate indicators and their associated standards, two questions were asked: What do we want the results of effectiveness to be? and What specific evidence are we willing to accept that the results have been achieved?

Each of the six critical success factors is described by indicators of effectiveness. The achievement of these indicators is the yardstick by which success is judged. Various collection devices are used to compile quantitative and qualitative results of the college's performance, and there are multiple processes for collecting data. Expected outcomes are measured in the following major areas:

- Assessment of academic major
- Assessment of student services
- Achievement in general education
- Criterion-based assessment
- Support of economic development
- Entry testing and course placement
- Tracking of student success through course sequencing
- Classroom research
- Retention to achievement of student goals
- Articulation and transfer
- Acquisition of public and private resources
- Facility adequacy
- Distribution of resources.

Each indicator of effectiveness is measured against a corresponding set of criteria, formally known as standards. The institutional effectiveness process allows for constant renewal and revision of standards as an integral part of the process. Sources of MTC's success standards include existing national or regional criteria, accreditation standards, national competency exams, and empirical institutional data. Data from each of these sources are used to evaluate the standards for the indicators of effectiveness.

Improving teaching and learning is the real purpose of implementing an institutional effectiveness process. If data are collected, but not used for institutional improvement, then the college has not fulfilled its commitment to being a truly effective institution. Evidence that the college uses data to improve teaching and learning is important to making institutional effectiveness a dynamic change process. Therefore, MTC publishes an annual institutional effectiveness *Report Card*.

The *Report Card* represents a yearly update on the college's institutional effectiveness program and captures the most recent data on the results of collegewide assessment activities and effectiveness standards. This document includes progress toward the college's long-range goals and priority initiatives, institutional effectiveness standards, and other noteworthy accomplishments related to assessment. Also, the *Report Card* is used to document reports prepared for the Commission on Higher Education and forms the basis for reaffirmation of reaccreditation for several programs.

Internally, the *Report Card* is presented to the MTC Board of Trustees at its annual August retreat. It is distributed through all direct reports of the Executive Council and is made available to the entire college community. Externally, the publication is distributed to the college's legislative delegation and to other key community leaders. The *Report Card* forms the basis of the college's external *Community Report*, which is mailed to 5,000 members of the community.

Because the ultimate test of institutional effectiveness is the use of assessment data to improve the college, MTC uses its institutional effectiveness program to celebrate successful accomplishment of goals and to make essential changes in programs and services, including improving academic departments, improving teaching and learning, reallocating college resources, and planning for professional development activities.

Auxiliary opportunities are made possible by data assessment; for example, institutional effectiveness results are also used to select outstanding employees, publish kudos in newsletters, select employees to be honored by the MTC Board of Trustess, and send congratulatory cards.

The *Report Card* is used within the college, not only to recognize success, but to assist in allocating resources to allow positive change to occur. MTC encourages decision making to happen at the lowest level possible in the organization and makes its institutional effectiveness *Report Card* available to everyone who works at the college.

The strategic planning process occurs in a three-year cycle; therefore, every third year, an outcomes report is published giving longitudinal data that track the college's accomplishments over the last cycle. This publication, *Strategic Planning Outcomes*, presents essential information about any change effected by data collected throughout the college's three-year strategic planning cycle. Changes resulting from interventions used to achieve the long-range goals and indicator standards are described.

How Institutional Effectiveness Improves Programs and Services

It is important to keep in mind that institutional effectiveness is more of a process than an event. The education of our diverse student body is complex and does not easily lend itself to the quantifiable data, charts, and formulas demanded by the agencies to whom we are accountable. Snapshots of effectiveness information are often incomplete because they represent one moment in a perpetual journey toward becoming the kind of institution we affirm ourselves to be in our mission statement.

In this section, categories of activity were chosen to illustrate the use of institutional effectiveness data. These examples are not intended to be definitive, but rather illustrative of how MTC goes about measuring its effectiveness.

Client satisfaction. No matter how good we may perceive ourselves to be, the perceptions of our students and community are more important measures. Therefore, two of our critical success factors deal with these perceptions: enrolled students' satisfaction and retention, and alumni satisfaction and success.

The retention of students to goal attainment may be the community college's greatest challenge. In the opinion of our critics, we have not done a very good job with retention. The national average for retention from freshman to sophomore year is 52 percent, according to the American College Testing Association, and the graduation rate of community colleges using student right-to-know legislation definitions is 20-25 percent.

At Midlands Technical College, one of the most important of our 19 indicators of success is student retention. To measure this indicator, we have developed a longitudinal tracking system. The initial data revealed our retention rate to be 46.4 percent—below both the national average and our benchmark. Believing we should be better than average, we implemented a number of intervention strategies.

- In 1988-89, student surveys of satisfaction revealed dissatisfaction with registration and in-take processes. We formed two cross-functional groups of staff and students to redesign the registration process and make it more user-friendly.
- We implemented a number of measures—for example, interactive student orientation programs and several special freshman-year courses—to inform students on success strategies.
- We created entering student advisement centers on both campuses.
- And, we set application and registration deadlines to guarantee that students are in class on the critical first day of the term when faculty are laying the foundation for productive learning.

Our retention rate for first-time freshmen has increased by 10 percent over five years to 56 percent. Surveys reveal increased student satisfaction with these services at a 90 percent-plus satisfaction level.

Institutional climate. A work climate that encourages faculty and staff to give 100 percent of their energy to providing quality client services is essential as a college responds to increasing enrollments and declining budgets. At MTC, a key critical success factor is dynamic organizational involvement and development. We believe inculcating the desire for continuous institutional improvement is basic to long-term quality, and we offer this story. In 1991, a decline in state resources required that MTC reduce the college's operating budget by $2 million. Restructuring and the necessary budget reductions were guided by the institutional effectiveness process. We engaged the college community in a process to identify the programs and services that were least essential to achieving the mission of the college. One hundred twenty-eight functions of the college, from teaching to mowing the grass, were identified. College faculty and staff were asked to place an equal number of the activities into four quadrants, with one being the highest priority and four the lowest. They were encouraged to make their choices based on college priorities as reflected in the MTC institutional effectiveness program. All personnel and services reductions were made from quadrant four functions.

Student learning. The ultimate test of institutional effectiveness is assessing what and how much our students are learning. What value do we add to students from their point of entry until they exit our college? Some indicators of value added are: success of transfer students, placement of career program graduates, perceptions of employers of graduates, and quality of teaching and learning. We measure these major outcome factors on an annual basis. However, to improve these important outcomes we must assess and improve effectiveness at the classroom level, as the following examples illustrate.

- In the late 1980s, a longitudinal study of more than 600 students enrolled in developmental studies courses indicated that over 20 percent remained in developmental courses longer than one year, with some students remaining in developmental courses as long as three years. Further, our developmental studies faculty had agreed on a standard of having developmental studies students do as well in subsequent courses as other students. We fell short of that standard. As a result of less than positive institutional effectiveness data, several actions were taken. A leadership change was made in the chair of the developmental studies department. Under the leadership of a new chair, the faculty undertook a complete revision of the developmental studies curriculum, moving from a self-paced individualized program to a teacher-directed, tightly structured program with clear course objectives and required time frame for completing objectives in a series of courses in each subject area. In a recent study of time spent in developmental courses (fall 1992 to fall 1995), we found only one student in 6,000 remained in developmental courses longer than one year. During the same time period, student success rates in the follow-on courses, after exiting developmental studies, increased.

- In 1992, the success rate for students enrolled in math courses was 65 percent—for example, 35 percent or 470 students each academic year were unsuccessful in this one course. The math faculty agreed that this was an unacceptable statistic. They collected multiple measurements of aggregate and classroom data to track students' progress through the prerequisite courses into the college algebra course and discovered missing and duplicate content in the curriculum, as well as instructional methods that were more suited to students for subsequent courses. They upgraded the curriculum in prerequisite courses and required departmental exit exams of all faculty. As a result, two years later in academic year 1994-95, the success rate in college algebra was 79 percent—a significant improvement.

Lessons Learned and Conclusions

Midlands Technical College's comprehensive institutional effectiveness program of planning and evaluation ensures that the college will exceed the criteria of the regional accrediting body and the South Carolina legislature's accountability mandates. But more importantly, the college is responding to the needs of its students and community. To do anything less would be unacceptable.

When the college seeks to recruit a student body, establish accountability with government and funding agencies, or establish its reputation as an essential community partner, there is nothing so profound as citing actual data that confirm the college's effectiveness—data that provide quantifiable proof that students are achieving their goals and finding successful careers. Beyond the necessity of meeting accountability mandates is the satisfaction derived from proving that the institution has achieved true success.

To a large measure, achieving community trust centers on institutional credibility. The concept of trust is paramount, and it is invaluable to colleges to present accountability information in a structured and orderly format.

In our quest to establish a workable institutional effectiveness process, we have learned a great deal about ourselves as an institution and our expectations. After almost a decade of using institutional effectiveness data, we offer some observations about the lessons we have learned.

Institutional effectiveness is a journey, not a destination. It is a dynamic process that continues to change as new information becomes available. We have learned from implementing the process, and we continue to make improvements along the way.

Trustee support and involvement are important. Since an institutional effectiveness program is mission driven, the board of trustees must understand and encourage the process. The board controls the resources essential to a successful program of institutional effectiveness.

Executive leadership is essential. The president and the college's executive leadership team will set the standard for the institution. Without leadership from the top, a comprehensive accountability program will not be sustained.

Faculty participation is integral to the enhancement of teaching and learning. Unfortunately, many educational accountability and total quality management programs focus on administrative procedures. To accomplish positive change in student learning and success, faculty must assume leadership roles and become active participants in classroom research.

Data must be used for improvement not punishment. A positive organizational climate that uses data for recognition and reward promotes collegewide participation.

Patience is essential. Perfection is not attainable because institutional effectiveness is a learning process. As implications of the results of various evaluation components were discussed, the college's leadership broadened their expectations of what the process could accomplish.

Flexibility and change are critical to the success of the process. Methodologies and data collection techniques have to be continuously reviewed, revised, and strengthened.

We are inspired by our vision, driven by our goals, and measured by our standards. We believe the view is definitely worth the climb. The institutional effectiveness movement offers a significant opportunity for community colleges to affirm their worth to our communities and collectively to our nation. However, there are no guarantees. The rewards of institutional effectiveness will mirror the intensity of effort put to pursuing and demonstrating it. We are challenged to seize the opportunity.

BACKGROUND

Midlands Technical College (MTC) in Columbia, South Carolina, is a multi-campus, comprehensive community college. The college has the third-largest under-graduate enrollment in the state with credit headcount of approximately 10,000 stu-dents each fall term. The continuing education enrollment is in excess of 25,000 annually.

The MTC institutional effectiveness model began its evolution in 1987 in con-junction with the college's reaffirmation of accreditation with the Commission on Colleges of the Southern Association of Colleges and Schools. MTC was one of the first colleges in the Southern region to adopt the new outcomes-oriented accreditation process. The college has since been chosen by the South Carolina Commission on Higher Education and the Kellogg Foundation to lead a consortium of community colleges in developing models for measuring their effectiveness. The MTC model has been widely recognized as successful in accomplishing its intended purpose. Its use and improvement of this process since 1987 make it one of the most seasoned in the institutional effectiveness movement. We at the college who have lived with this process believe it is a sound, effective way to approach a very complex task. We view our planning system as an opportunity for renewal.

Community College Press has just published *Managing Your Institution's Effectiveness: A User Guide,* prepared by Midlands Technical College. To order, call 1-800-250-6557.

REFERENCES

Bullen, C. and Rockart, J. *A Primer on Critical Success Factors*. Cambridge, MA: Center for Information Systems, Massachusetts Institute of Technology, 1981.

Crosby, P.B. *Quality Is Free*. New York: New American Library, 1979.

Ewell, P.T. "The Assessment Movement: Implications for Teaching and Learning." In O'Banion, T. (ed.), *Teaching and Learning in the Community College*. Washington, DC: Community College Press, 1994, 73-96.

Harvey, J. and Immerwahr, J. "Goodwill and Growing Worry: Public Perceptions of American Higher Education." *The Fragile Coalition: Public Support for Higher Education in the 1990s*. Washington, DC: James Harvey and Associates, 1995.

Joint Commission on Accountability Reporting. *Technical Conventions Manual for Reporting Accountability Information*. Washington, DC: American Association of State Colleges and Universities, 1996.

Southern Association of Colleges and Schools. *Criteria for Accreditation*. Atlanta, GA: Southern Association of Colleges and Schools, 1991.

Marchese, T. "Accountability." *Change*, November/December 1994, 26 (6), 4.

Chapter IV

Although the Community College of Denver (CO) initially began work on its institutional effectiveness model more than a decade ago, it was not until 1993 that the college first described the processes that it was implementing to measure and evaluate its effectiveness. As at Midlands Technical College, an annual planning cycle selects priorities for each academic year and drives planning throughout CCD.

The model that Byron McClenney, CCD president, outlines in the chapter is admittedly developmental—by design. The college annually describes where it would like to go, the action plan for the following year reflects the "developmental gap," and the next year's plan is drawn. No more than five priorities are targeted each year, all drawn from the updated strategies or visions that emerge from the annual planning cycle. In addition to other effectiveness data publications distributed in and out of the college, a special report, Achievements/Results, *documents the outcomes of all pursuits of college strategies and priorities.*

Accountability reporting has become routine and the norm; as case in point, effectiveness data describing college progress in improving student achievement are even published in the college catalogue. Selected effectiveness strategies currently being implemented at the college are described in this chapter, as are some of the benchmarks reached in the college's pursuit of excellence.

Byron McClenney
President
Community College of Denver
Denver, Colorado

PRODUCTIVITY AND EFFECTIVENESS
AT THE COMMUNITY COLLEGE OF DENVER

The way to gain a good reputation is to endeavor
to be what you desire to appear.
—Socrates

Until the North Central Association of Colleges and Schools (NCA) evaluated the Community College of Denver (CCD) in October 1993, the processes used to measure and evaluate the institution's effectiveness had never been fully described. The threads of these processes, however, had been woven through CCD's planning and accountability activities, thus creating the fabric of the final effectiveness model.

The origins of the CCD approach date back to 1986, when faculty and staff were asked to respond to a variety of possible goals for the future development of the institution as an activity of their annual convocation. Some individuals were surprised, some were skeptical, but they all dug into the task of rating goal statements. The results of that rating activity were printed in the first internal newsletter for the new academic year. The discerning reader could see that CCD had agreed on a vision of the institution—an institution where students would come first and where collaboration would be the manner in which work would be done.

As follow-up to the 1986 convocation activities, a representative group (designated as the Planning Council) was asked to conduct what today might be called an "environmental scan" of the service area and to take a hard look at the movement of students through the institution. A series of background papers was developed by appropriate faculty and staff members. These papers were distributed to all personnel with the indication that they would be the basis for the spring 1987 convocation, where faculty and staff would meet in small groups to discuss the papers' implications. The groups produced tentative strategies on how the college might move forward in light of what had been learned about the institution and its service area. The Planning Council took the results of these discussions and created the first set of strategies for the future and priorities for the next year. This cycle of activity quickly became institutionalized into an annual cycle that has allowed the faculty and staff to learn from the results of the previous year and to plan the next steps in developing the type of institution they envisioned.

The internal discussions at the college were reinforced by the Colorado legislature's mandate of an accountability program for public higher education in 1988. The mandate to implement the program went to the Colorado Commission on Higher Education (CCHE), which functions as a coordinating body for the state's 28 public institutions of higher education. The CCHE decided that each institution was to develop its own unique plan and structure for an annual report on institutional progress. The first year was to focus on planning and development; the annual reports in subsequent years were to focus on achievements. During the second cycle of reporting, institutions recognized by the CCHE as exemplary in measuring effectiveness were allowed to move from writing a lengthy report to making a brief summary of the annual update. The faculty and staff of CCD were rewarded for their early hard and effective work by being included in the first group of four to be so recognized.

A combination of internal initiatives launched in 1987 and external mandates emanating from the legislative action in 1988 provided the fuel and foundation for an evolving effort at CCD. Further impetus came from the expectations for institutional accreditation. An emerging focus on the assessment of student outcomes by the NCA simply reinforced what already had become an institutional priority. A decade-long journey to create an effective college was under way.

The Process
The major points of external validation for this comprehensive process came in 1991 with CCHE affirmation and in 1993 with NCA affirmation. The feedback from the regional accrediting body provided the encouragement to continue the coordinated development of the processes for accountability and planning. Today, a given year's priorities drive planning throughout the institution and are critical to moving the college in the desired directions. A comparison of the 1988 priorities with those of 1994 and 1997 illustrates that as the college community has become more comfortable and familiar with the approach, the types of priorities have shifted significantly.

> **1988 Priorities** • Public relations/image • Assertive at Auraria campus • Access for students • Programs that address community needs • Salaries • Professional development • Improved communication
> **1994 Priorities** • Holistic plan for advising • Faculty effectiveness • Student retention • Efficient student services • Celebration of diversity

1997 Priorities • Fostering student success • Improving instructional delivery • Improving faculty effectiveness • Celebrating diversity • Defining rights and responsibilities of faculty and students • Building community and collaborating • Coordination of information technology

The priorities targeted each year are all drawn from the updated strategies or visions that emerge from the annual cycle. Special background or issue papers and other relevant documents have been important sources of information for implementing the process. In recent years, the council also has turned to the college's *Accountability Report* as an important data source. The *Report* supplies the council with specific information about general education skills and knowledge; discipline-specific skills and knowledge; retention and completion; student, graduate, alumni, and employer satisfaction; and student performance after graduation. These supporting data provide a strong base for the strategies and priorities produced by the council.

Each year a different group of individuals meet and form the Planning Council to make sense of student and institutional performance data. Convocations and open forums are utilized to engage people beyond the work of representative groups. The hope is that the systematic evaluation of accountability, assessment, and planning information will routinely lead to improvements in program delivery and student support.

As part of CCD's commitment to evaluation, the 1996 college catalog included, for the first time, "Excellence Through Accountability," a special report to inform the public about progress in improving student achievement. The following representative items illustrate the manner in which information is reported:

- Ninety-six percent of current and graduating students are satisfied with the teaching they have received.
- Ninety-nine percent of alumni and employers surveyed are satisfied with the skills of CCD graduates.
- Ninety-eight percent of graduates who prepared for employment are in the labor force or continuing their education.
- The yearly number of successful students (graduation or transfer) has increased by 98 percent in the last decade.
- People of color comprise 42.5 percent of the successful students.
- Transfer students from CCD have an average GPA of 2.9, which is equal to or higher than the native students in the universities to which they transfer.

Moreover, the *Schedule of Classes* for each semester now includes summary reports based on surveys of currently enrolled students. The levels of satisfaction experienced by current students create expectations for prospective

CCD students and for the faculty and staff. The message that the institution wants its students to be satisfied and successful is reinforced strongly.

The Institutional Effectiveness Model

When the CCD institutional effectiveness model was first described in 1992, it simply detailed an annual cycle of activity through which the institution had moved each year since 1987. Subsequent work in 1995 and 1996 refined the approach to link accountability and planning in order to build a more effective community college.

Simply put, the model encourages a process of learning from the outcomes of the previous year; of developing strategies and priorities; of planning for the next year by responding to the strategies and priorities; and of allocating or reallocating resources on the basis of the resulting plans. The model actually creates a developmental gap between what the institution says it has done and where it would like to go. The gap then is filled by the action plan for the next year.

The vision, projections, and strategies extend beyond the operating year and help keep the focus on what might be possible if plans are implemented successfully during the coming year. For example, the vision created at the end of 1996—for 1997-1998 and beyond—included the following:

- The college will employ advanced informational and instructional technology to provide state-of-the-art learning, teaching, and working opportunities.
- Success rates of students of all races, classes, and cultures will be comparably high.
- All employees will be trained in customer service and computing.
- CCD will be a model institution offering education that is accessible, affordable, and appropriate for the needs of its service area.
- CCD will increasingly use systematic environmental scanning, futuring and continuous quality improvement in its planning processes.
- Internal and external customers will be satisfied with the learning and working environment.
- CCD will be a leading provider of customized and contract training.

The collection of data, the synthesis of reports, and the production of the *Accountability Report* provide the feedback needed by the Planning Council to update strategies and identify priorities for the next year. Once these products are available, each unit and area of the institution is expected to initiate discussions leading to a plan for the next year. The resulting plan always includes the achievements and results for the current year; desirable outcomes for next year; projections for the second year and beyond; and priorities for personnel, equipment, and projects. Unit plans (e.g., arts and humanities division or financial aid) are combined into area plans for instruction, student services, administrative services, campus centers (Technical Education Centers), and president's staff.

There are severe page limitations on the documents produced at each level; no section can exceed two pages. The discussion among faculty in a division or among vice presidents before the final college plan emerges leads to clarity and consensus about the choices to be made. The last level of review and consolidation results in the overall college plan. Line-item budgeting does not begin until the plan has been circulated and leaders have had a chance to make adjustments to their respective unit plans.

One of the most powerful and compelling examples of how the process can produce results over a multiyear period can be found in the pursuit of diversity. Each year since 1987, CCD has had a priority that dealt with some aspect of diversity. Recruitment, retention, graduation, and celebration have emerged annually as common themes; and the expectation has evolved that all units will seek to contribute to the pursuit of each of these priorities. The cumulative impact has been dramatic. The institution has doubled credit enrollment and moved from 27 percent minority enrollment to 54 percent in a decade. More dramatic than the steeper pitch in the trend line are the successful outcomes that have been achieved. As just one more example, minority student success for this decade moved from 13 percent to 42.5 percent of the total number of students graduated or transferred to a four-year college.

Key to such improvements is that special populations are routinely included as part of the quest for accountability. The discovery that one group is not performing as well as another is a significant motivator for change. In particular, feedback about individual programs provides grist for important discussions by faculty in individual divisions.

The cumulative impact of repeating the cycle of activity each year over a 10-year period has changed the way the institution operates dramatically. The college has developed a new way of conducting business. There is an annual redefinition of the college's vision, followed by a disciplined effort to move the entire institution in desired directions. Professional development efforts undergird that movement. Mini-grants reinforce individual projects that aim to achieve institutional goals, with the full involvement of the Teaching/Learning Center. Illustrations from 1996 will help explain:

- The college funded 27 faculty mini-grants to support an innovative curriculum and expanded uses of technology.
- A total of 1,028 (duplicated head count) faculty and staff participated in 126 Teaching/Learning Center workshops, including 22 on diversity or multiculturalism and 40 on technology.
- There were 10 dialogues on diversity led by "Boundaries and Borderlands."

In any given year, the college's strategies and priorities are pursued by numerous processes and activities, but the outcomes of all of these are reported in a special publication, *Achievement/Results*. For example, outreach priorities led to the creation of the Technical Education Centers (four sites) and further development at one of those centers. Priorities on student success led to cost control in the administrative areas so that dollars could be allocated to student support. After the expansion of the campus centers, the administrative costs as a percentage of the budget remained at or near the bottom in comparison with other community colleges. Priorities drove the way the institution sought grant support, and collaborative efforts resulted from priorities focused on partnerships.

The college's board of trustees monitors the processes with a keen eye on the institutional vision. Whether a proposed budget moves the institution in the desired direction—and then whether plans are actually implemented—are items the board routinely monitors and oversees. The annual cycle of activity includes the board, which monitors the ongoing progress in institutional development and effectiveness. Occasionally, other factors are brought to the board's attention. For example, in a recent review of presidential performance, the board received a report based on results of an anonymous survey of all college personnel. The survey indicated that 84 percent of faculty and 96 percent of administrators believe the institution effectively plans and then allocates resources on the basis of plans.

The CCHE affirmation on accountability results and the NCA evaluation provide the board summative assurance of the quality results achieved and provide further evidence to all constituencies that CCD is holding fast to its vision—being an effective community college.

When an eight-member accreditation evaluation team from the NCA visited CCD to reaffirm accreditation and evaluate institutional effectiveness and accountability, their report indicated they found "a college that had put in place exemplary planning and accountability activities." In addition, they discovered that "accountability and effectiveness measurements are part of the college fabric"; and they were impressed by the quality of the annual update processes. Other evaluative comments in the NCA report demonstrated the quality of the institution to students and the community, including:

- "The college clearly has a commitment to support students and promote successful outcomes."
- "[A]nalyzed results are used to formulate budget priorities, improve instruction, maintain academic standards, and improve advising systems and services to students."
- "CCD has indicated that it takes very seriously the state mandates on accountability and the NCA mandate on assessment of student academic achievement."

- "Frankly, the team was pleased to evaluate a college that undertook the planning/accountability/assessment activities in the spirit in which they were meant. The college decided to take a look at itself and to improve."

Lessons Learned and Conclusions

A number of overarching principles have emerged over the 10 years CCD has been actively pursuing demonstrable effectiveness.

- It is important to have a collegewide commitment to ongoing internal and external assessment.
- It is important to identify critical or strategic issues through assessment activity.
- Research efforts should be scheduled to provide data and information at the appropriate time in the annual cycle.
- A base of useful information must be developed for planning from all of the available data.
- The credibility of the people translating data into useful information (the Planning Council) is crucial.
- Strategic thinking should be seen as guiding operational planning (next year) and operational planning as guiding the allocation and reallocation of resources.
- There is a need to develop and enforce a plan for planning, including a simple format to achieve it.
- Institutional decision making should be focused on addressing the critical issues.
- Incremental budgeting is at odds with the developmental processes of the annual cycle of activity.
- The budget should implement the important values.
- The initial development and the annual updates appear equally important. (If the energy of the organization is focused on student success, for example, then an annual cycle that reinforces the important next steps with data-driven updates can produce enormous changes in ways an institution relates to clients.)

CCD recognized early that the collective vision and values of the institution need to be at the core of all institutional effectiveness processes. With the institution's vision and values in the forefront, a real transformation can occur. The cumulative impact of each unit of the institution learning from the experience of the previous year and using that learning as the springboard for planning the next year produces a significant ongoing movement. If overarching concerns focus on student achievement and success, then individuals in the institution can make plans each year to improve success rates.

CCD faculty and staff now routinely expect feedback about course completion rates; semester-to-semester retention; year-to-year retention; success of students exiting remedial courses; graduation rates; transfers to four-year institutions and subsequent success; pass rates on licensure examinations; student satisfaction; employer satisfaction with graduates; placement rates for graduates. What is learned in a given year is reported to the public and utilized to plan for improvements. Each year the bar is raised as more is known about the areas needing improvement.

Public reporting is an area in which the institution continues to learn. The use of the *Annual Report* for accountability reporting has become routine, and publishing the "Excellence Through Accountability" report in the catalog and summarizing student surveys in the class schedule have shown promise. The public response has been positive, and legislators seem pleased to see an institution taking seriously their mandates calling for greater accountability.

The people of CCD have reached the point where they do not fear being measured. They have been involved for a decade in determining the standards against which these measurements can be made. Faculty routinely make clear to students what they should know and be able to do as they exit courses and programs, and they routinely plan for new interventions to help more students be successful. In short, they are willing to be held accountable.

As a result of the efforts reported, CCD has reached the following benchmarks:

- The institution has become the most diverse among colleges and universities in Colorado.
- The institution has had the highest percentage of increase in graduates in Colorado for three years.
- The institution has the highest percentage of successful minority students of any college or university in Colorado.
- CCD students who complete remedial courses are as likely to graduate and/or transfer as other students.
- Approximately 40 percent of CCD degree-seeking students either graduate or transfer to four-year colleges.
- The average GPA of CCD transfers is equal to or higher than the native students in the four-year institutions to which they transfer.
- The institution has become the leading point of entry to higher education for citizens of the city and county of Denver in spite of intense competition for students.

CCD has worked hard to create a student-centered, self-examining institution, characterized by collaboration. If there is any magic in the CCD approach, it is in the tending of the annual cycle of activity. Overt efforts are made each year to link resource allocation to the purposes, vision, and values that have been developed through a shared struggle to create an effective community college. The processes are ongoing because the people of CCD choose to be a part of a developing institution. After a decade of progress, the Community College of Denver continues to look ahead and to grow. As this is written, the bar is already being raised for 1997.

BACKGROUND

The Community College of Denver's (CCD) primary service area is the city and county of Denver with a population of approximately 500,000. Ethnic minorities make up approximately 40 percent of the population-at-large and 66 percent of the student population in the Denver public schools. The institution is unique among community colleges in that its home base is the Auraria Higher Education Center, which also houses Metropolitan State College of Denver and the University of Colorado at Denver. More than 33,000 students are served on the large center city campus. In addition, CCD operates four campus centers in the poorest neighborhoods of Denver. Another site incorporates the Continuing Education division, and over 10 sites are utilized for adult basic education. Workplace education offerings are scattered throughout the service area.

CCD serves an unduplicated credit head count enrollment of 11,000 and many thousands more in numerous diverse services. Credit enrollment changes every day, due to extensive open-entry/open-exit, self-paced offerings. Approximately 25 percent of all college courses are offered in this manner.

Credit enrollment has doubled during the past decade. Minority student enrollment has grown from 27 percent to 54 percent of the total. The number of graduates has doubled, and the trend line has a steeper pitch than the enrollment trend line.

Chapter V

Midlands Technical College and the Community College of Denver provide, principally, broad-brush descriptions of faculty and staff involvement with the design of their effectiveness plans. But, in this chapter, Pat McAtee, president of Cowley County Community College (KS), focuses his primary attention on the collaborative processes by which all members of the college worked with local business and industry, others in the community, and other colleges to identify the critical pieces of an effectiveness model, and then took ownership of the final plan.

At the heart of CCCC's planning is the implementation of a continuous performance improvement (CPI) process, by which the college prioritizes accountability issues within a cost-effective, employee-driven approach to its own management. A management team administers college business, and a Quality Leadership Council (QLC) oversees responses to quality issues and guides the activities of process-improvement and cross-functional teams. The detailed process of defining institutional purpose and effectiveness described in this chapter illustrates well a college's commitment to and persistence in creating a model that reflects the unique characteristics and needs of the institution—a major criterion for success. These descriptions make valuable reading for institutions seeking to implement the initiatives drawn from the philosophies of total quality management and continuous process improvement.

Patrick J. McAtee
President
Cowley County Community College and
Area Vocational-Technical School
Arkansas City, Kansas

EFFECTIVE STEWARDSHIP: MAKING THE CASE FOR MEASURING OUTCOMES AND ACCOUNTABILITY

We shall not cease from exploration, and the end of all our exploring will be to arrive where we started and know the place for the first time.
—T.S. Eliot

Community colleges across the nation face an increasing expectation of greater accountability to constituents. In Kansas, and especially at Cowley County Community College and Area Vocational-Technical School (CCCC), a customer-service attitude has driven efforts to use available talent and resources to develop and implement an institutional effectiveness model that satisfies the demands of program evaluation, outcomes assessment, and funding accountability. As we implemented the model, we asked two key questions that guided and informed the process: "What do our customers need and want?" and "What must we do to be effective in our response to these needs?" In the sections that follow, the systemic and internal process that contributed to the college's resolve will be detailed, providing the context for a description of the process that was used to develop the model. Finally, the model itself will be outlined and a number of key lessons detailed.

Systemic and Internal Pressures

In today's Information Age, a well-educated workforce is crucial to the ability of any company to compete on a global level. Computer technology itself is no longer the focus of change. Technology is now a tool for disseminating information throughout the world and bringing rapid change to the global marketplace and culture. The changing global economic structure brings a new kind of excitement and opportunity to the community college, but also increasing pressure from national, state, and local sources. Accountability is the watchword of the 1990s: Government demands justification for the funds it provides higher education, accrediting bodies seek demonstrable quality in programs and services through measurable outcomes assessment methodology, business and industry demand a literate workforce, and taxpayers seek a guarantee for personal education dollars and time spent in training. With funding for education becoming tighter at all levels, simply stating the curriculum is no longer enough. Programs and services must be appropriate, be cost-effective, and have results corroborated by outcomes assessment.

This anecdotal story illustrates the response of Kansas community colleges, and most especially that of CCCC: There once was a woman who was shopping around for an advertising company to serve her company's needs. She called three different agencies and simply asked, "What time is it?" The first agency responded, "According to our operating procedures, it is 12:00 p.m." The Second company said, "We will research that and get back to you." But the third agency said, "What time do you want it to be?" She chose the third advertising firm. Cowley has made a commitment to emulate the attitude of the third advertising firm. To answer the diverse needs of the population served, the college must respond appropriately and effectively to pressures from within the institution and expectations from outside—national and regional, state, and local.

National and regional pressures. The federal role in community college management is not markedly different from its role in all of higher education. Federal mandates, such as the Americans with Disabilities Act and affirmative action and civil rights legislation require institutions seeking federal funds to comply with federal regulations. Accompanying the pressures of federal regulations is a plethora of national trends and reform efforts. Partnerships with public schools can draw community colleges into initiatives such as National Skills Standards, Tech Prep, and School-to-Work. Linkages with business, industry, and other employment and training agencies, such as Job Training Partnership Act and welfare job training programs, involve the college in certification and other processes; one-stop career centers; and employee testing, placement, and follow-up. Guaranteeing graduate satisfaction with the education acquired and community college consumer reports are other national reform trends to be investigated. And, finally, the importance of the pressure from accrediting agencies and federal efforts cannot be overlooked.

State pressures. The line between coordination and control is finely drawn at the state level. State mandates regarding programs and services provided might well restrict efforts to provide services for constituents. State-level coordination focuses attention on regulations under which community colleges operate, moves decisionmaking to broader political arenas, and fosters the development of administrators whose chief responsibilities are to interpret codes. The positive impacts of these moves are more-stable funding, more services for certain groups of students, higher standards of operation, and less program duplication. It is too early to say if these pressures are a general benefit or a detriment, but such statewide involvement certainly changes the ground rules for institutional operation, the professional outlook of the staff, and how the college is perceived by the public.

In Kansas, the major impact on community colleges comes primarily from two state entities: the legislature and the Kansas State Board of Education (KSBE). The Kansas legislature is charged with allocating funds for all levels of education in all types of schools and colleges within the state. This task can be difficult for individual legislators who have limited experience or knowledge of community colleges or their philosophies. These limited experiences may explain the decrease in community college funding from the state level in Kansas over the last five years—despite the fact that the cost per student increased during the same time frame (Table 1).

Revenue sources	89-90	90-91	91-92	92-93	93-94	94-95	95-96*
State funds	31.0	30.35	27.72	27.72	27,72	28.00	28.40
Student costs	11.58	14.47	16.16	16.20	17.76	19.23	19.76

*estimated

Table 1: Revenue Sources—
State Aid and General Fund Plus Vocational Fund %

Currently, only 1.7 percent of all dollars budgeted for education in Kansas go toward funding community colleges (Timmer, 1995). As a result, all Kansas community colleges are primarily credit-hour-driven and depend heavily on local mill levies. Cowley, for example, receives only 37 percent of its operating budget from state funds.

In an effort to meld community colleges into a statewide system, the Kansas legislature has established accountability standards, staff and program development guidelines, and program definitions. To address concerns about cost effectiveness and program quality, the legislature has asked each community college to develop a policy that defines institutional effectiveness and identifies the indicators that will be used to confirm accountability. The crucial determinant for state-level decisionmaking is based upon what is *best for the system* rather than what is best for a particular college. Some have suggested implementing statewide coordination of community college institutional research to make uniform data available. At present, Kansas community college technical programs are required to submit formal enrollment data, placement follow-up data, and employer follow-up reports to the KSBE. Noncompliance may result in a reduction or loss of funding—or even program closure.

Local pressures. Creating cost-effective options for all Cowley students is critical to the long-term success of the institution. The reality of decreasing state funding poses great challenges to the college as it strives to serve the diverse needs of local constituents. Adding to these challenges are local pressures that keep the college focused on measuring effectiveness. These fall into four categories: institutional responsibilities to the taxpayer (the most important); trustee responsibilities to the college and community; business and industry training priorities; and students' educational needs.

Taxpayers. Education competes for taxpayer support with a broad range of societal priorities that appear in local, state, and federal budgets. As these resources are spread across more programs, community colleges must somehow find ways of doing more with less. At the same time, constituents want services and programs that answer changing employment needs. In Cowley County, residents who are struggling to adjust to the harsh economic realities of plant downsizing, declines in agriculture, and slow growth in retail sales look to the college and to area industrial leaders for direction, help, and leadership to solve regional economic challenges. Still, taxpayers in the county can be counted upon to resist any attempt to raise mill levies or increase their personal tax burden to pay for innovation. The expectation is that the college will work to solve regional problems, but will also somehow absorb the costs of keeping programs and services on the cutting edge of technological change.

Beyond the traditional roles of offering cultural events, continuing education, and educational enrichment, area residents also expect Cowley to assume a leadership role in community development. It is expected that the college will assist economic efforts to attract new businesses, offer specialized training to produce high-quality employees, and participate in community service.

In the past eight years, plant closings, layoffs, and management reorganization in area corporations have posed challenges for the entire service area. Taxpayers look to CCCC to provide access to job-market information, connections to support services, continuing analysis of human resource needs, and futuristic planning for the service area. In response to the taxpayer expectations, the college is evaluated and held accountable for the economic health of its service area.

Board of trustees. Ideally, the board of trustees serves as a bridge between the college and community, translating community needs for education into college policies and protecting the college from untoward external demands. As institutions become more complex, board members must respond not only to more initiatives from constituents within the college, but also to monitoring and controlling agents outside the college. Leveling enrollments, reduced state and local funding, public skepticism, and slowness to change are just some of the issues community college trustees face. Ultimately, the board of trustees is accountable to the taxpayers who support the institution and expect quality outcomes for tax dollars spent.

Business and industry. CCCC has enjoyed a good relationship with area business and industry for many years. The partnerships that have emerged from these relationships, while clearly positive forces, have nonetheless created pressures for personalized training and retraining, as well as a demand for assistance in identifying job skill sets, employee assessment and placement, and employee screening, referral, and recruitment. Because of industry's voracious appetite for state-of-the-art, high-tech training and remedial education, business leaders have become increasingly involved in the education process. They serve on school-to-work, tech prep, and advisory committees, and are working with the college to help identify potential worker competencies. Working with area high school and community college educators, business and industry leaders are influential forces in the process of delineating and facilitating the *identification* of job readiness competencies and *validation* of specific vocational-technical competencies. When brought into the planning process, area business and industry leaders have high expectations regarding the results of their efforts and are conscientious in their follow-up.

Students. Economic turmoil is a powerful stimulus spurring disadvantaged, undereducated, and underskilled area residents to return to school for services such as GED, basic skill development, technical/vocational skill training, and retraining opportunities. In turn, these programs have swollen with students that are diverse in culture and needs. CCCC, like most community colleges, maintains an open-admissions policy and the influx of underprepared students challenge the legitimacy of program outcomes. Whatever skill levels students bring upon entry, they must meet program outcomes to be certified. To accomplish this, instructional programs, testing and counseling services, course content, and performance requirements must all relate to a shared vision of desired competencies and outcomes. Certificates and degrees must be the concrete evidence that predetermined, specific proficiencies are achieved at some minimum level.

Only 12 percent of area residents hold bachelor's degrees, contrasted to 21 percent statewide. Over 25 percent of the college's service area population have no high school diplomas, compared to 18.7 percent in the state. For these students, CCCC may be the only opportunity for basic skills development and successful negotiation of college or technical courses. Given these challenges, Cowley has reached out to area secondary schools and other two- and four-year institutions, developing partnerships to address more completely the numerous regional needs. Cowley works to facilitate a smoother transition from high school to community college to four-year institutions through articulation of courses, elimination of duplicated coursework, better use of resources, and programs in tech prep and school-to-work.

The net result of these four sources of pressure is the expectation that Cowley will promote excellence without producing excessive economic demands on the tax base. The demands within the service area are especially intense and represent an ongoing challenge for the college.

The Process

At Cowley, long-range planning encompasses the view that institutional purpose and effectiveness is a continuously evolving process. Over the past few years, this process has been enhanced by the implementation of a continuous performance improvement process (CPI)—a process that serves as a vehicle guiding the college's long-range planning and outcomes assessment processes.

Development of the CPI concept was an outgrowth of a focus on continuous quality improvement (CQI) that had taken root in business and industry within the college's service area. In spring 1990, the college began to reach out to institutions and businesses that were exploring or implementing CQI and CPI processes. At the same time, 400 leaders from the industrial, educational, and service sectors formed the Two Rivers Quality Improvement Network (TRQIN) to address economic growth issues of the region. Simply stated, TRQIN's mission was to help bring the total quality management/continuous performance improvement processes to local communities to help develop and educate a workforce capable of competing on a global basis. From the beginning, CPI appeared to be a cost-effective, employee-driven approach to managing an organization—and a viable process for prioritizing accountability issues being emphasized by state and federal funding sources and accrediting agencies.

By spring 1991, faculty in-services were devoted to increasing individual awareness of CPI. Courses in CPI were also offered to area business and industry personnel. Subsequent requests from business and industry for more courses were so numerous, that by spring 1993 the college had committed two full-time faculty members to facilitate continuous performance improvement courses and to initiate a two-year program of study in quality improvement processes.

A Train-the-Trainer workshop for college support staff was held, and the college began a series of short-term quality improvement seminars (culture, teamwork and statistical-process control) for support staff in June 1993. During the same semester, college administration and trustees were introduced to quality improvement processes in a three-day seminar. In July 1993, the Quality Leadership Council (QLC) was established to provide leadership, support, structure, and channels of communication for quality issues identified by college personnel.

At that point, a committee was named to determine the direction the college should take in designing and implementing a plan of institutional effectiveness. A 15-member Planning, Assessment, and Community Excellence (PACE) committee was formed with representatives from faculty, staff, administration, and the board of trustees. PACE committee members collected a range of information through faculty and staff in-services, advisory committees, meetings with business and industry leaders, and recommendations from cross-functional and process-improvement teams. These data were compiled and analyzed by the PACE committee to help develop a new college mission statement, institutional commitments, goals, objectives, and outcomes assessment activities.

The new mission, which states that the college is "an open-access institution [that] seeks to empower individuals with broad-based and proactive skills in order to compete and perform on a world-class level," provides an overall direction for the entire institution and represents a consistency of purpose for process improvement. The college's nine critical goals—which address institutional commitments in academic life, student life, community service, support services, and ethics, are a synthesis of collegewide and community consensus about the college's current identity and future directions that will position CCCC as a quality institution into the twenty-first century. The revision of the college mission was a long, arduous process, and was originally undertaken as preparation for the North Central Association's (NCA) accreditation review. All levels of college personnel were involved in the experience through a variety of CPI teams. The mission statement follows a form consistent with recent recommendations from the North Central Assessment Plan Review Panels.

The PACE committee also made progress toward the establishment of an institutional effectiveness model and program competencies. Subsequently, small institutional groups further discussed academic competencies, student outcomes, a system to assess student skills and competencies, instruments and procedures, and a review of outreach courses and programs.

The institutional effectiveness model that emerged provides a structure through which new ideas can be brought to the attention of the entire college community and fine-tuned through process improvement teams; the resulting recommendations are transmitted through the QLC to the rest of the institution. The subsequent improvement, if accepted, is implemented and a follow-up evaluation is conducted.

Institutional Effectiveness Model

Cowley's institutional effectiveness model, illustrated in Figure 1, is firmly grounded in and driven by the college's mission statement. The model consists of four major structural components: the board of trustees, the president, the management team, and the Quality Leadership Council.

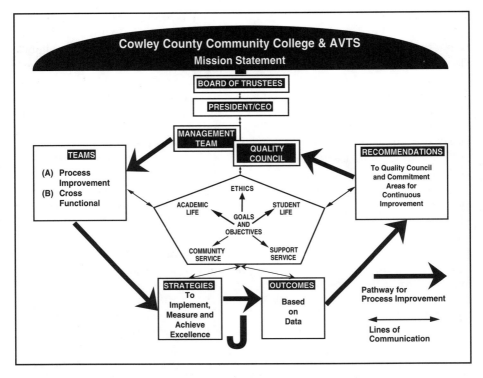

Figure 1: Institutional Effectiveness Model—
A Process for Continuous Performance Improvement

Through this structure, quality initiatives are proposed and refined using a CPI approach.

With the institutional effectiveness model as context, the CPI process encourages a constant review and evaluation of goals and objectives; if deemed no longer relevant, they may be changed or eliminated. As part of the assessment portion of the model, each party responsible for meeting an objective responds to a questionnaire regarding the progress that has been made to fulfill the accompanying plan of action. After consultation with team members, that party reports as to whether the objective has been completed, what actions were taken to complete the objective, whether the objective is to be continued in the next long-range plan, and what modifications are needed for the next plan. This process ensures that goals and objectives do not become paper dreams to be read and filed away. Review and evaluation by various process-improvement or cross-functional teams can also be applied to the mission and/or commitments; however, these components generally have remained constant.

Foundation—the institutional mission. The institutional mission statement, commitments, goals, and objectives purposefully focus on student learning, but the mission gives direction for *all* improvements made at the college. All levels of college personnel are aware of the college's purpose and understand that a quality workforce needs continuous improvement in technical and general education and guidance for balancing work and leisure.

The effectiveness structure and CPI process. The board of trustees and the president are committed to using the CPI process to accomplish the mission of the college and have established two key groups to provide leadership and to address emerging issues. The management team and Quality Leadership Council (QLC) are largely composed of the same individuals; the QLC adds two TQM/CPI coordinators. The management team deals with the day-to-day business of administering college business; the QLC deals only with quality issues.

The QLC's task is to coordinate and implement the CPI effort. Its members are individuals with access to and responsibility for information and knowledge of the entire college; they provide oversight and long-range vision for collegewide change and growth. Quality initiatives by the process improvement team are not exercises in "business as usual," nor are they free-for-all activities. Management still manages, but from a different perspective. The process of team management becomes more of a coaching or guiding activity rather than a series of directives. Each team moves through a formal seven-step problem-solving process. Four of the steps involve meetings with the QLC where feedback, focus, and refocus are provided. The seven-step process addresses seven critical elements in improvement that encourage a continuous loop of communication. They are:

- To define and clarify the project
- to identify the current condition with available data
- to analyze the most likely causes for the condition
- to select a solution and plan of action to apply
- to implement the plan
- to evaluate the improvement
- to standardize the improvement.

Two types of teams work to address college objectives. Process-improvement teams, initiated at the division level, are usually guided by the leader of that function and address improvements within a specific area. These quality initiatives may be proposed by any faculty or staff member of the college. Cross-functional teams (initiated by the QLC) address processes that affect the entire institution. Both process-improvement teams and cross-functional teams have specific purposes and goals, and their activities are guided by the QLC. Teams set up strategies to implement action plans for the area under review, develop measurable outcomes for the plans, and submit their ideas to the QLC. Near the end of the process, the teams' recommendations, if accepted by the council, are implemented formally. The improvement is evaluated and standardized, if appropriate.

Each process or cross-functional team formally reports on the status of that group's project at four specific points: the definition and clarification of the project, the analysis of problem causes, the solution to the problem, and the implementation of the plan. During each of these steps, the responsibility of the QLC is to ensure that the focus of the project remains consistent with the institution's mission, commitments, goals, and objectives. Because the QLC is involved at key points in the activity, there are fewer unexpected outcomes from the problem-solving process at the end of the project.

Communication and information-flow patterns are indicated in Figure 1 through single lines that represent communication pathways and heavier arrows that indicate how improvement ideas move through the institutional structure. Lines of communication are always open, and the flow is in both directions. Continuous improvement ideas move in a circular pattern, fine-tuning the proposed improvement until a consensus is reached. This continuous, fluid exchange of feedback allows information to flow in many directions at once, at all times, and at all stages of the continuous process improvement activity.

Recommendations that affect only one area are passed from process-improvement teams to the specific functional area for implementation. Recommendations that affect the total organization are made to the QLC, which provides coordination and implementation. The result is continuous improvement. The decisions made by each team, each functional area, and the QLC are intended expressly to fulfill the mission of the college. The process is a key element in the college's ability to meet and exceed customer expectations throughout the organization and address both internal and external pressures that relate to accountability, performance funding, and effectiveness.

Cowley's institutional effectiveness model provides a framework to allow both internal and external customers to see how the college documents, analyzes, and solves issues, and how it responds to challenges faced by the institution. The process is a standardized, consistent, and dependable way to justify the spending of tax dollars.

Outcomes assessment. No division, or even institution, has the resources of time, materials, or funds to assess all aspects of each degree program. Nonetheless, at Cowley, assessment priorities focus on continuously improving the quality of the college's educational services and offerings. To this end, the college emphasizes quality and outcomes by adding assurance procedures that include standardized syllabi; division, department, and program reviews; telephone surveys of students; student services surveys; and advisory data from the community.

Beneficiaries. The institutional effectiveness practices that CCCC's model of institutional effectiveness describes are intended to benefit the college's internal and external customers. Specified goals, objectives, and outcomes help faculty measure the effectiveness of instruction. These same measures also help ensure that CCCC students attain the necessary skills to live, work, and contribute productively to society. National and state accrediting agencies (the North Central Association, the Kansas legislature, and the Kansas State Board of Education) have mandated that institutions demonstrate their effectiveness. These agencies, the public, and our customers are vigilant in the expectation that Cowley County Community College and Area Vocational-Technical School will produce students that perform well in all areas, including core skills, communication, leadership, adaptability, personnel management, group effectiveness, technology knowledge, and human and social skills.

Lessons Learned and Conclusions

A number of major lessons were learned though the development and implementation of CCCC's institutional effectiveness model.

The model will not work unless the entire organization accepts ownership. In addition, there must be a mechanism by which faculty and staff can be made aware of salient information from national, regional, state, and local sources for the planning process. In order for this to occur, the institutional climate must be receptive to change, but such receptiveness rarely occurs naturally within any organization. Length of time in an organization solidifies the old ways of doing things. Many people cling to what they know best and can be resistant to new ideas that force them to leap into the unknown. Only by thoroughly understanding a new vision can the individual process of buy-in begin to work. In the beginning of the process at Cowley, it was often necessary to force people to step outside their personal comfort zones and experiment.

Before a feeling of ownership can occur, extensive input from the administration, board of trustees, faculty, staff, students, and community must be sought. Both positive and negative inputs are vital to the process of acceptance. Prior to the implementation of any change, the administration and board must commit to the change process itself and take a chance on a new approach. Some have to give up control for the greater good of the institution. Both administrators and board members have to recognize that the way things had been managed in the past is not necessarily the most effective way to manage them in the future. Enthusiasm among CCCC's administrators and board members for a new management model was, ultimately, the engine that drove the development of an institutional effectiveness framework.

The pursuit of effectiveness is highly dependent on the level of honesty with which people address the process and the challenges presented through that process. To bring the entire faculty and staff on board, a number of issues had to be addressed, beginning with the issue of trust. The administration had to trust that faculty and staff were interested in improving the institution; the faculty and staff had to believe that change was not just another word for "more work, no help" and accept the empowerment offered. A new perspective was required of everyone. Only when employees truly felt that their ideas and opinions could have a direct impact on college policies, programs, structures, and procedures did they begin to feel free to explore a variety of quality issues and promote effective solutions. The process of achieving that level of trust began with education and constant reassurance that faculty and staff input was important. This was not always easy to achieve. For example, the institution discovered it was much easier to get the organization excited about a new path of quality than it was to maintain enthusiasm for the journey. As in any organization, skeptics always exist and must be convinced to accept empowerment and ownership in the new paradigm. Some within the institution still believe there are better strategies out there to encourage more ownership in the model.

The development of the framework required more time than anticipated. Business and industry leaders, service area constituents, and college personnel were invited to be involved in changing the college management paradigm, and soon it was clear that the process would take months rather than weeks. The delay was put to good use, however, allowing the institution time to begin educating and empowering college personnel to become involved in the change process. The biggest challenge during this period was to resist the temptation to assign the model development to one or two people to speed up the process. Fortunately, multiple sources of input and a demand for consensus within the leadership consistently won out over expediency.

The rigor associated with the implementation of any new change limits the successes and progress that can be seen on a daily basis. To the casual observer, the college may often look as though nothing has changed. It is important to keep in mind that the road to success is rarely a straight line. A change in the administration or board can affect the implementation of ideas and processes. Nonetheless, the overall process must somehow remain visible and become a daily part of why the institution exists, not just a set of dusty documents nor the exclusive property of the administration. Encouraging ownership is hard because it is so easy to become mired in the day-to-day details of running a college and serving students. For this very reason, it is vital to avoid the temptation to leave the process in the hands of the administration after input from various sources has been gathered.

The real work begins after the model is developed. Unfortunately, at that point, many in the organization feel like the work is already done. Involvement and enthusiasm must be fueled through constant reminders of the institutional vision. Ultimately, an organizational vision can only be established and maintained through the efforts of everyone involved.

Continuous training is a must for all involved in the organization, especially the leadership. This training must include everyone—administrators, faculty, and staff. At CCCC, new employee orientation has developed into a comprehensive and ongoing effort.

Not all of the issues, no matter how important, can be addressed at once. At Cowley, formal meetings with the teams and the ongoing guidance of the QLC allowed for continuous communication, training, and understanding of each individual team's direction. When the effectiveness model was first implemented, teams established mission areas that were too broad and ambitious; the groups tried to cover too much. Teams that could not complete their improvement projects in a relatively short time floundered and lost enthusiasm. The key to efficient coordination and consistency of effort was to limit the charges given teams from the start, thus allowing more of them to complete their tasks successfully in a reasonably short amount of time. This allowed two important things to happen: the number of tasks completed increased, and the quality of recommendations and solutions was enhanced. Serious work remains to be done, however. Among the issues still to be addressed are teaching loads, the number of meetings faculty and staff must attend, and confusion about the difference between a division work group and a quality process team.

The process of defining the new model for institutional effectiveness promoted reflection on ways to improve the planning process so it might also serve to keep the institution's programs and services on the cutting edge of information technology. The institution discovered that traditional indicators of institutional effectiveness such as retention, job placement, and graduation rates were not the only indicators that needed to be considered in an effectiveness plan. The 1996 faculty in-service stressed that market awareness, speed of response to perceived customer need, and customer satisfaction were also important. The need for systematic progress reports and numerous correction procedures was emphasized, and those using the model were asked to strive to reflect consistently the highest priorities of the institution and avoid wasting time on issues that could be more appropriately addressed later in the process.

In the beginning, the process was much too lengthy and encompassed more than college personnel could carefully monitor. The importance of narrowing objectives in short-term planning to make appropriate use of available resources was quickly discovered. Many felt that there were too many objectives to address and measure effectively. The QLC reviewed the mission, commitments, goals, and objectives in a systematic process to ensure that they could appropriately be monitored. As a result, the commitment to community service was divided into two new commitments: community enrichment and economic development. Such continuous analysis of goals and commitments was essential.

Measurement and assessment of outcomes are still under discussion. Some within the institution believe more time and creative thought should be given to the measurement phase of the institutional effectiveness model, that the college uses far too many surveys. Surveys have provided useful information, however. For example, a questionnaire of more than a hundred business and industry CEOs, community leaders, and educational constituents from the service area revealed some impressive outcomes, as well as honest responses about areas that need improvement. Prior to choosing a survey, it is important to ask: "Why am I collecting this data?" "What am I trying to measure?" and "What changes will be brought about to improve the institution as a result?"

Perhaps the most important lesson learned is that any effectiveness model must be custom-designed to fit the needs of the college. Many institutions have good effectiveness models, but no single approach is appropriate for every institution. Examining effectiveness models from business, industry, government, and education was helpful in the development of our model, but CCCC's effectiveness model had to be based on the particular needs of our institution, our community, and our local business and industry.

The Cowley effectiveness model is based on the philosophy of total quality management and continuous process improvement. In its development, we studied the work of most of the recognized quality leaders before settling down to the long, hard process of developing our own plan. We worked closely with local business and industry, the community, and other colleges to ensure that our model was geared to meeting the needs of our customers. We educated our faculty and staff about the impending change in institutional philosophy and management style. We developed a method of following up on goals and objectives to ensure appropriate action was taken. Change became less threatening, and the goal of encouraging excellence in ourselves and our students was clearly affirmed through the team process. Local community leaders also became aware of this desire for excellence and freedom of expression, openly providing feedback on the institution's outcomes measures and performance indicators. The team approach to planning and assessment made it much easier to measure institutional effectiveness. The model that emerged from this process is by no means perfect, nor is it finished. When an institution commits to a future-oriented, continuous process improvement management, there is always room for quality improvements.

The author gratefully acknowledges the contributions made by the employees of Cowley County Community College and Area Vocational-Technical School who make this process work, and especially those of Susan Rush, director of assessment, and the writing team.

BACKGROUND

The broad mission of Kansas community colleges is to provide equal access to quality educational programs and services, at low cost, to those who may benefit. While this mission has enabled Kansas community colleges to better serve a wider and more diverse set of customers, each new role ultimately adds to the entangled web of groups to whom the Kansas community college is accountable.

Cowley County Community College and Area Vocational-Technical School was originally established in 1922 as Arkansas City Junior College, operating under the jurisdiction of the Board of Education of the Arkansas City Public Schools. In July 1967, a separate board of trustees was elected by the citizens of the county and given full control of the operation of the community college and area vocational-technical school. Currently, while governed by the elected board of trustees, all community colleges in Kansas are under the jurisdiction of the Kansas State Board of Education.

Arkansas City, home of the main college campus, is a rural community of 15,000 people located in south-central Kansas, 60 miles south of Wichita and three miles north of the Oklahoma border. In the beginning, CCCC was fondly referred to by alumni as "Basement U" because of its location in the old Ark City High School. Since 1922, the college has grown from 60 students enrolled in a limited liberal arts program to nearly 3,200 students currently enrolled in expanded general, occupational, continuing education, and business and industry programs. In addition to a modern main campus, the college has established numerous outreach centers including sites in Wichita, Winfield, Wellington, and Mulvane.

Customized business and industry training is a major focus of college services, and enrollment in this kind of training has grown from 3,000 contact hours in 1990 to more than 159,000 contact hours in 1996. Major industries located in Cowley County and served by the college include units of a number of Fortune 500 companies such as a General Electric small jet engine repair facility, Rubbermaid, Inc., and Binney & Smith, the Crayola division of Hallmark, Inc.

Cowley employs 126 full-time faculty, staff, and administration, and 310 part-time faculty, staff, and student workers. Although campus housing is available for 258 students, most students commute to the main campus or one of the 15 outreach centers. The college offers 32 certificate and applied science programs and 36 liberal arts/transfer programs. Developmental coursework is available for students requiring skill-building in English, reading, and math. A number of special programs are offered, most notably for senior citizens and displaced homemakers. CCCC is a community-oriented, customer-focused, service institution committed to discovering the needs of constituents and developing services and programs that will meet those needs.

REFERENCES

Timmer, G. "Fiscal Year 1996 State General Fund." Presented to the State Board of Education by director of the budget, state of Kansas, September 12, 1995.

Chapter VI

Walter Bumphus, president of Brookhaven College (TX), directs primary attention to a single college's implementation of continuous quality improvement (CQI) principles within the larger structure of its district's commitment to the implementation of CQI initiatives. He reports on Brookhaven's five-year journey of folding concepts from the quality movement into the development of the institutional effectiveness model.

The principles of CQI—systems thinking, management by fact, and continuous improvement—are personalized at the college by cross-functional teams, broad-based planning, and systematic project team development. The model and effectiveness processes used to plan, implement, and assess outcomes are illustrated using specific programs and activities currently in operation at Brookhaven. A major example of the college's daily commitment to CQI is its extremely successful Quality Initiatives program—where more than 300 employees, over the past five years, either individually or in workgroups, have elected to look closely at what they do and how they do it, investigate how the quality of what they do can be improved, take steps to make that improvement, and then report the results of their efforts to the larger body.

Walter Bumphus
President
Brookhaven College
Farmers Branch, Texas

DEVELOPING AN INSTITUTIONAL EFFECTIVENESS MODEL: CONTINUOUS QUALITY IMPROVEMENT AT WORK

Those organizations that have made quality their most important goal will live to fight another day. Those that haven't chosen quality as their goal face an uncertain future.
—Daniel Seymour, *On Q: Causing Quality in Higher Education*

Brookhaven College has a history of innovation and success, but it has not escaped the changes and pressures of its external operating environment. A downturn in student enrollment and reduced state funding have accompanied increased pressure to prove college effectiveness to the taxpayers, to the board of trustees, to the United States government, and to the Texas legislature. The college has discovered that it must address and satisfy significant external concerns—for example, the state's share of funding for community college education decreased from 61 percent of total revenue in 1985 to 46 percent in 1995; and the funding shift from state support toward more local revenue bases has brought greater scrutiny of outcomes by the board of trustees—for example, concern over increasing operating costs in the face of a declining student population and directives for more cost-effective approaches.

The demands of governmental and accrediting agencies also influence college operations. A series of external effectiveness mandates have ensued—including the Texas Higher Education Coordinating Board institutional effectiveness process (a required, comprehensive strategic plan which is assessed annually against standards and measures, and which includes a peer review every four years), the Access and Equity Plan for compliance with state and federal requirements, the Americans with Disabilities Act, and the institutional effectiveness criteria established by the Commission on Colleges of the Southern Association of Schools and Colleges (SACS).

In addition to the direct demands from the various external agencies is the strong indirect influence of what amounts to a fundamental revolution occurring within the Texas workforce education system and welfare system. What has been an unwieldy conglomerate of 28 Texas workforce programs spread among 10 state agencies is now being folded into the Texas Workforce Commission. This commission will certify local workforce boards which will control the flow of funds to educational institutions for work-related adult training. The intent is an employer-driven, universal system, serving all citizens. The challenge to Brookhaven College in this environment is to reposition itself as a very attractive "best buy" for the limited time and training funds of individuals within the system (Hammond, 1996). The college's capacity to document and prove high value for dollars spent is crucial to its ability to compete.

Declining resources exacerbate the systemic and external pressure to greater accountability. As funding has become more precarious and limited, stewardship of available resources has driven the initiatives for greater effectiveness and brought about increased scrutiny at the federal, state, and local levels. A different type of institution will evolve from the responses to these pressures. This new institution will focus on learning and partnership, both internally and externally.

The Larger Context

More than six years ago, Texas and Dallas County—as did most other states and major metropolitan areas in the U.S.—began to focus on building a skilled workforce in the interest of economic development. Simultaneously, the Dallas County Community College District's (DCCCD) seven independently accredited colleges were approaching self-study and reaccreditation. While continuous quality improvement (CQI) had been in various stages of implementation in American companies and organizations for almost two decades, it was just gaining the attention of the public sectors of education in the mid-1980s, primarily as diminishing resources were pressuring educational leaders to reduce administrative expenses through improved efficiency and effectiveness—outcomes of the CQI processes. While not directly transferable to this sector, the principles could be adapted and modified to improve the ways in which institutions of higher education did business.

The district and the colleges looked at CQI as a vehicle for planning, analysis, and continuous improvement activities, and as a management strategy for providing better service to students, the community, four-year colleges and universities, and others. Its definition of CQI helped focus attention on broad and complex concepts:

> [CQI is a] set of theories, practices and tools that use leadership, systems thinking, quantitative methods and team empowerment to improve an organization's capacity to meet and surpass current and future customer needs. (Johnson, 1995, p. 16)

As early as 1991, the district began CQI training for various service areas and became a charter member of the continuous quality improvement Network (CQIN). For the next four years, a number of events emphasized an ongoing commitment to CQI principles for planning, implementation, and evaluation. In 1992, continuous improvement teams were formed at various locations throughout the district; in 1993, Brookhaven College and Richland College joined CQIN, and the position of director of quality and planning was created at the district level; a quality advisors group was formed in 1994, and CQI awareness training began for new DCCCD hires. In 1994, a final sentence was added to DCCCD's purpose statement, reflecting the district's strong commitment to the implementation of continuous quality initiatives.

Since 1991, Brookhaven College has been moving toward CQI operations, folding concepts from the quality movement into the development of the institutional effectiveness model. The principles of CQI, integral to the college's drive to meet the challenges posed by the rapidly changing environment, have helped the college embrace and address a myriad of institutional effectiveness activities designed to respond to the challenges and pressures of the external environment. They are:

- **Systems thinking**. Understanding work as a system so it is apparent where focused effort is needed
- **Management by fact**. Using data and knowledge of variation to know how the organization is performing
- **Continuous improvement**. Using an organizational process to improve the outcomes of the work processes (Johnson, 1995, p. 16)

The college's CQI implementation plan, drawn in 1991, included the following foci for the subsequent three academic years:

- **1991-92**: leadership commitment to CQI; steering team trained; general awareness training for staff; quality initiatives program launched
- **1992-93**: general awareness training for support staff; specialized training for faculty; quality initiatives program expanded, quality teams initiated, quality unit added
- **1993-94**: focus on expanding faculty training; statistical process control training for college management; customer service training for support staff; strengthening outcomes emphasis in quality initiatives program (Johnson, 1995, p. 17).

The Process

Brookhaven College believes in the value of strategic planning and outlines, within the plan, broad boundaries for actions and priorities. Goals are developed directly from the mission and vision statements, and represent desired outcomes related to the college's institutional effectiveness targets. The college operates with a two-year planning cycle; goals and priorities are written, reviewed, and adopted during the first year of each cycle. Activities and individual action plans are developed at the workgroup level to support appropriate goals and priorities.

Planning and evaluation are ongoing processes. A coordinated planning process emphasizes continuous input and evaluation by the college community. Employees at all levels are actively encouraged to take part in the development of the plan, its implementation, and evaluation. These processes directly and indirectly affect staff and the students they serve. An essential part of the college's planning effort is regular assessment and recording of the results of the initiatives implemented by the college during the year to achieve its goals. Each goal is carefully assessed to determine the college's overall effectiveness with regard to its stated mission and purposes. Summarized findings of this annual review are available to the college-at-large.

Operating within this participatory management style, decisions are reached through broad-based involvement. Input is solicited through brainstorming sessions with faculty, staff and students, through regularly scheduled meetings with employee groups and informal dialog opportunities with the president. Additionally, the college makes fact-based decisions which rest on a foundation of regular and ad hoc institutional research and data reports. External factors, such as changes in technology, demographics, and market sensitivities, are reviewed and considered in the process of making decisions.

The model and processes the college uses to plan, implement, and assess outcomes will be illustrated through a series of examples including the planning of a one-stop student services center, an academic coordinated studies program, the college's quality initiative program, the institutional effectiveness planning and related activities, the staff development system within the college, and the implementation and operations of the Teaching and Learning Center. The processes include the development of cross-functional teams, broad-based planning, and systematic project team development.

The Student Services Center. Perhaps one of the most notable examples of how the college teams have improved services is the process model used to design and build the college's new Student Services Center. In the spirit of CQI, the college charged a cross-functional team to benchmark exemplary student development operations across the nation. This team conducted field research through site visits and ultimately proposed a construction design model where form followed function. As a result, the college has a state-of-the-art, one-stop student-centered facility that houses all intake services as well as the business office, student programs office, cafeteria, bookstore, and job placement operation.

Attention was paid early on to function before form; that is, it was important to discuss with the potential users of the facilities what their specific needs would be. Brainstorming sessions identified the various functions of the building; as a result of these cross-functional collaborative efforts, the functions were described as:

- to serve as the entry point to the campus
- to house all of the pre- and post-enrollment service offices
- to enhance the quality of campus life for student.

The next phase of the planning process included benchmarking, management by data, and cross-divisional collaboration (Thomas, 1995).

Benchmarking. Once the vision, functions, and form of the building were established, the benchmarking team visited campuses that had one-stop shop facilities and was charged specifically with making observations about student traffic flow, floor plans, accommodations of the registration process, and building design. Gathering information from nine college campuses in three states assisted in designing the Brookhaven building.

Management by fact. The team conducted on-site interviews at each of the visited sites, identifying how the facility accommodated the various institutional processes, how the students flowed through the process, and what the floor plans and the building design concepts looked like. Interviews helped the team identify the major challenges that had to be considered in the initial design of the building. The team made observations based on their knowledge of the respective areas, as well. They recorded their visits with photographs and videotapes, which were reviewed and analyzed later as the project developed. A "living document" developed from which the team could draw in the design phase of the building (Thomas, 1995, p. 20).

Cross-divisional collaboration. After the benchmarking process was completed, the president identified focus groups to be involved in the design phase. The focus groups were to identify and prioritize the primary users of the building by divisions. The CQI tool of "light voting" was used to prioritize the identified functions and the users that would occupy the building. The following functions were identified:

- admissions/registrar
- bookstore
- cafeteria
- continuing education
- counseling center
- financial aid
- health center
- international center
- job placement
- Project Excel

- services for special populations
- testing center
- student programs and resource (Thomas, 1995, p. 21).

The last step in the design phase involved all of the division managers and staff in identifying the locations of each of the functions, as well as the likely flow of student traffic. Students were included in the design processes of student, office, and lounge space. The vice president of student development coordinated meetings with the design architects and division managers to develop the schematic of the building. The design was ready well within the construction time frame, and the entire Brookhaven College learning community had been involved in the college's efforts.

Coordinated studies. Collaboration between faculty from various disciplines offers students a program each semester in which a range of subject matter is studied from the perspective of a common theme or with a common focus. This program has been even more successful since the introduction of CQI into the classroom. Students and faculty utilize these tools to present material, lead discussions, work collaboratively on projects, brainstorm, look at issues in new ways, and assist in classroom management.

An integral part of Brookhaven's institutional effectiveness plan is providing for the development of its human resources, the key to any organization's vitality and long-term success. No organization can be better than the collective talents, skills, and abilities of its members. Brookhaven College has a long-standing commitment to nurturing and developing its employees through a wide array of educational opportunities. These include special staff development opportunities that focus on teaching and learning, technological changes, and other areas to improve the quality of virtually all educational services.

Brookhaven College's staff development plan is designed for the whole college community—faculty, administrators, and support staff. The comprehensive offerings represent a holistic approach to personal and professional growth. The 1995-96 program included more than 200 sessions developed around eight organizational core themes: orientation, CQI, leadership, health and safety, professional growth, enrichment and professional renewal, supervision and management, and technology.

Teaching and Learning Center. Dedicated space and operational dollars allow staffing and administration of a Teaching and Learning Center to further emphasize the development and growth needs of full-time faculty and adjunct instructors. Sessions covering teaching innovations and new technological approaches are offered. The center offers adjunct instructors electronic mail and Internet accounts, and provides technologically sophisticated computer equipment to aid in the production of instructional materials.

External consultancy. Consistent with the college's commitment to CQI, staff have worked to provide workshops on CQI principles for external organizations. They have served as process consultants for other organizations exploring the effectiveness of their current operations. For example, the college reviewed and audited the local chamber of commerce's vision and mission statements. The college played an important informal consulting role as the chamber's objectives of re-aligning its priorities and restructuring the responsibilities of key staff and volunteers to better utilize resources were realized.

Improved registration system. The college has developed a successful strategic management system for a computerized, student-driven registration process. We wanted to modify the registration and to move from "doing things right" to "doing the right things!" (Burke, 1995, p. 22) In an effort to improve the registration process, a task force set about developing a strategy for revising registration and the enrollment/advising services. Registration at the time was being conducted in an arena format, with staff working at tables and students standing in long lines. Computer terminals were used for data entry, and transparencies on overhead projectors posted the classes that had been closed or cancelled. Moreover, registration periods were limited, and "time permits" controlled for the numbers of students that could be admitted into the registration area.

A benchmarking team traveled to eight colleges in three states; one of the team members observed that the experience was not a "paradigm shift" but rather a "paradigm earthquake" in his thinking about the registration processes (Burke, 1995, p. 23). A second team was charged with using the generic recommendations from the benchmarking team to focus specifically on registration. They were to:

- design the ideal model for registering Brookhaven students
- move toward the concept of a one-stop shop for students
- streamline registration in all phases of the process
- identify strategies
- create a timeline for implementation
- determine locations/space/support needed (Burke, 1995, p. 23).

Team members represented multiple campus and district services. A survey of staff, faculty, and students provided additional perspectives. The team created a timeline for:

- development of a registration philosophy statement
- development of registration parameters
- design of a model system
- timeline for implementation field tests, pilot system, full implementation
- ongoing evaluation, analysis, and modifications
- implementation at the district level (Burke, 1995, p. 23).

The development of a philosophy statement, considered crucial to the implementation of future registration decisions, required the team to wrestle with their various perceptions of registration and how the system they developed would fit with others on campus. Moreover, the team was to identify the registration parameters; it approached these parameters as the identification of "quality issues." Several CQI tools were used in this effort, including the plus/delta activity. This is a method of conducting an evaluation, for example, of a process or a proposal. The connotation of "plus" is positive, and "delta" connotes the need for change. It is a method of looking at the positives and negatives of the activity being analyzed and can be used as a summative or a formative evaluation activity; it is, however, always an interactive group process, with group members calling out pluses and deltas to create a list of items for eventual discussion by the entire group.

With the design of the final model decided, recommendations were made to the president and the campus; the recommendations addressed the quality issues, established implementation goals, and identified the cross-campus implications of changing the existing registration system, including the need for interdependence of campus systems to make the new model operate at its greatest potential. Three years and thousands of hours were involved in changing the registration system, but the final product has since been the catalyst for similar efforts at other colleges in the district, as well as for the evaluation of other processes and systems at both the campus and district level. College staff and faculty credit the CQI process with the success of their efforts.

Quality initiatives. The college does not view continuous quality improvement as a panacea. It is a proclamation of the pride we have in our college. It is a covenant we have made with both our internal and external customers to focus on quality and to give our best every day. An example of this daily commitment is the college's Quality Initiatives program. Quality initiatives are "activities based on analysis of ideas, concepts, and perspectives of the work team...intended to improve the quality of work output through improvement of the work process...[and] can simply be a part of a small incremental change" (Bumphus, 1995, p. 35).

Since its inception in 1991, the Quality Initiatives program has annually involved more than two dozen workgroups across the campus representing more than 300 employees. Through this program, staff are encouraged to look closely at what they do and how they do it to see how the quality of services can be improved. Workgroup initiatives are identified in the fall and are attended to throughout the year. The benefits to the organization are evaluated at the close of the fiscal year (or at the end of the initiative time frame). Evaluation occurs around five quality criteria:

- quality of work and/or educational environment improvement
- enhancement of services

- cost effectiveness
- longevity
- replicability.

Institutional effectiveness team. While looking at processes from a quality perspective, the college is also aware that external and internal changes are demanding more performance accountability. These include the emphasis on institutional effectiveness through state agencies and accrediting bodies. The president selected the members of the institutional effectiveness (IE) team to include broad-based involvement and representation of all work and employee groups. The majority of the team members were faculty. Using CQI tools, the team engaged in an exploration of IE models, measurement tools, and processes. The results of this exploration provided a framework by which Brookhaven College could meet the Southern Association of Colleges and Schools' mandates for an IE program, as well as the Texas Higher Education Coordinating Board's requirements. Additionally, it satisfied the college's own desire to assess and report its accomplishments with a wide range of important outcomes. Based on their research, the team prepared information for distribution to the college community—a brief history, rationale, definitions, approaches to implement IE, plans for fall 1994 and spring 1995, and an explanation of the role of the committee.

In the past, the college had looked at what it was doing (mostly in response to state reporting requirements) in a general way, usually conducting talleys but not addressing the quality of its efforts. It became evident when conducting the self-assessment for accreditation through the Southern Association of Colleges and Schools that a process should be developed and implemented to provide for systematically gathering and reporting data—a process that would determine whether the college was achieving its mission. While the primary reason for instituting a college institutional effectiveness plan and process was self-knowledge, external pressures influenced the timing of its development and implementation.

In alignment with the college's commitment to CQI, a participatory process to design the IE model was developed by the institutional effectiveness team to ensure ownership in the process at all levels. Rather than responding to a mandate from top administration regarding appropriate measures, divisions and departments were asked to identify indicators that should accurately reveal how well the college was doing. Using this strong foundation, the IE team began its work of developing the collegewide core indicators of effectiveness.

Institutional effectiveness process. Based on the experience of working with the Quality Initiatives program, the institutional effectiveness team decided that IE planning and implementation should be a collegewide activity. This required that the divisions and departments serve as the foci for activity. In the tradition of continuous quality improvement, the institutional effectiveness team modeled the belief that the people involved in the process know how the process works best and how to measure the outcomes most effectively.

During fall 1994, team members met with all divisions and departments and shared the results of the committee's research with the college community. Each division and department was asked to develop core indicators of effectiveness and assessment plans for their individual areas. Implementation manuals were provided to each work group. The manuals included definitions, samples, suggested processes, assessment tools, lists of readily available reports, and other resources. Members of the IE team made themselves available to act as resources as needed during this process of development and refinement. This process ensured that "counting what counts" would begin at the very roots of the institution and would only take final form through broad-based input across every college activity.

The institutional effectiveness model. The institutional effectiveness team agreed with Packwood (1990) that the success of the college, not individual departments or divisions, should be the concern of faculty and staff throughout the institution, and that they should be involved in identifying appropriate measures and implementing them in their own programs and services. Not only did the workgroups provide the indicators from which the collegewide indicators were developed, but the college community was utilized as a resource for feedback, clarification, and input along the way.

The college team developed five core performance indicators and 15 performance measures. Single performance measures for each of the five core performance indicators are listed here to provide representative samples:

- **Subsequent course performance**. Performance in college-level courses by ESL and developmental students.
- **Satisfaction with and increased utilization of college support services**. Student ratings of pre-enrollment, enrollment, post-enrollment, career counseling, business office, student programs, and instructional services.
- **Degree and certificate completion**. Number of students completing degrees.
- **Performance beyond Brookhaven**. Employer satisfaction ratings.
- **Market penetration**. Enrollments by percent of households in service area and in Dallas County for credit and non-credit courses.

It is important to note here that the DCCCD monitored seven categories of performance indicators during the 1995 academic year. Brookhaven College's five core performance indicators were established and monitored (in addition to those required by the district). Many of the district indicators reflected a strong external perspective of providing the community with valuable and needed services. Each of the following examples provides one of several indicators in each of the seven categories:

- **Career preparation**. Number of business needs surveys completed; and related programs instituted, refined, or canceled as a result
- **Transfer preparation**. Number and percent of DCCCD students who indicate intention to transfer and do so (irrespective of DCCCD credits earned)
- **Continuing education**. Number and percent of surveyed students and employers indicating satisfaction on occupational and job skill upgrades
- **Basic skills**. Success of developmental, GED, and ESL completers in college-level courses
- **Access**. Extent to which student body reflects Dallas County adult population (credit and non-credit)
- **Economic development**. Number of firms entering into training contracts with DCCCD
- **Citizenship**. Number of courses which incorporate community service into the curriculum.

An important part of designing an institutional effectiveness model is to ensure that the indicators are measurable. When the initial reporting format completed by divisions and departments was developed, two of the components included were the identification of performance targets and data sources. This model made available the regular reporting and evaluation processes that had been routinely prepared by each department, but not necessarily shared with the rest of the college. Identification of additional data sources was completed with the support of the college's data and research staff.

Except for a college support services survey and an employer survey, data sources are existing records and reports that are updated regularly. The college support services survey was developed by the IE team during early fall 1995 for administration in the late fall. The employer survey is still being developed at the time of this writing. Research support for program-level indicators is provided as needed by the Office of Institutional Advancement and Administration.

Data-gathering on workgroup-based performance measures and on performance measures for each of the five core indicators took place in spring 1996. The collegewide report, which will include progress toward the collegewide indicators as well as the division- and department-level indicators, will be completed and distributed during fall 1996.

Since the reporting process on core indicators of effectiveness has only begun at Brookhaven, the college is looking forward to the results from this year's assessment. The baseline data will allow determination of how instruction and services can be improved and provide a picture of the value-added to students. The data will be compared to the college's mission and goals to produce a composite picture of the college's effectiveness.

Lessons Learned and Conclusions

Higher education has survived changes in society for hundreds of years, but the pace of change challenges institutions to look at what they do in light of current realities.

> Voices from all quarters are calling for a reexamination of what institutions do and how they do it in the light of realities of the late twentieth century. In the minds of critics as well as many supporters, there is no reason why higher education should hold itself aloof from the need to serve customers, to supply wants rather than define needs, or to pursue and husband resources with the same assiduousness as other businesses. (Pew Higher Education Roundtable, 1996, p. 2)

Brookhaven College recognizes that examination of what it does is critical to its ability to survive. We have learned some valuable lessons along the way. Some selected "learnings" from *Reflections on Quality* (Crosby, 1996) serve as categories for a discussion of the lessons we learned so far in our quest for institutional effectiveness.

Crosby Reflection #113: *One of the myths of management is that meetings are a gigantic waste of time. Only poorly managed meetings are not useful.*

As has been illustrated and summarized here, numerous meetings were held to produce plans, foster implementation, and provide assessment of projects. We learned that it was important to have these many meetings to allow for broad-based participation in the process. We also learned that different types of meetings are scheduled for different purposes—and it is especially helpful to alert the teams to the type of meeting being conducted (for example, whether the meeting being scheduled is for idea creation, decision-making, or information-sharing).

Crosby Reflection #125: *The most difficult lesson for the quality crusader to learn is that real improvement just plain takes a while to accomplish.*

In the case of Brookhaven College, a new student services center was a dream for 10 years, a steady work-in-progress for two years, and a continuously improving facility since its opening two years ago. Similarly, it takes two to four years to build a "critical mass" of faculty and staff trained and practiced in CQI to begin meaningful, positive change. It takes a full 18 months to plan, prototype, test, and implement a new computerized student registration system. There simply are no quick fixes.

Crosby Reflection #180: *When you decide to change a culture, you had better be sure you know exactly what you are going to change—and why.*

Consider the major changes at Brookhaven College triggered by consolidating student services from over eight campus locations to one student-friendly facility. Without the creation of a shared group (team) vision, such a task can be very difficult. It is easier to become sidetracked and befuddled than not. Brookhaven College utilized several strategies to allow for the emergence of a team vision, most notably benchmarking and numerous focus and planning meetings. Teams traveled to several model colleges to learn first hand what they wanted and did not want within the scope of this major project. The benchmarking teams shared their findings with their campus colleagues via video, written reports, and verbal descriptions. This vision was shared with district planners, architects, and contractors. Literally thousands of person-hours later, the student center is remarkably close to the original college team vision of improving student services.

Crosby Reflection #199: *Relationships are where it all comes together or comes apart. Nothing else can be made to happen if relationships do not exist.*

No significant achievement at Brookhaven College has been made without the work of effective teams. It takes considerable time to build teams, and each team member must have made a real commitment to reducing any "rugged individualism" for the betterment of the work teams. For example, the coordinated studies faculty built remarkably effective relationships as they co-designed the curriculum, lessons, materials, and lectures for the coordinated studies program. The Teaching and Learning Center faculty and staff have pulled together to provide innovative and supportive services to the college community. The list providing examples of effective teams goes on and on, yet the principle remains the same: Team relationships, built one person at a time over time, with the emergence of shared vision, is the way everything comes together.

Brookhaven College has enjoyed a full measure of success leading to healthy pride and optimism. Students perform well on standardized tests, perform well upon transfer to senior institutions, and serve local business and industry to their satisfaction. Yet, as with most other colleges, Brookhaven has faced and will continue to face a multitude of pressures to improve. The examples used here to describe our progress have included several of the college's most recent significant successes. The institutional effectiveness model, the principles of CQI, and other organizational development principles help the college meet its challenges.

What is past is past. Successes of the past are a great foundation, but today Brookhaven is challenged to continue the task of improving on the very successes we have described here. To that end, the president recently charged new teams to begin work on developing the visions and relationships they believe are required to meet any needs that have been neglected to date. These new teams are developing plans and strategies for such diverse initiatives as exploring niche and segment marketing, developing a one-stop career center, providing exemplary student and community access to internet-based services, improving student retention, and developing world-class workforce education.

Brookhaven College is forging a new partnership between faculty and administration with the goal of producing learning whenever, wherever, and however it best serves the students, the community, and the community's employers. Widespread dialogue, shared budget information, demographic trend and forecast data, support for experimentation, and a vision of a collaborative college provide impetus for this partnership.

The college is moving toward mass customization, attempting to identify the most cost-effective means of serving its varied constituencies. Simply put, the college seeks to identify similar needs and characteristics of the diverse groups within its student body, and to coordinate the findings with the development and/or scheduling of programs to meet the larger customer base. Indicators of the value of this approach include the recent successes of short semesters, the long-term success of industry-based programs, the high retention rate within the program for first-generation college students, and the development of new business and agency training partnerships.

Finally, the college, as are many of its corporate and industrial community partners, is moving toward a market-driven model of "time-based competition," characterized by a service orientation that demands it adapt schedules, facilities, programs, and products to student needs, community demands, and business interests. Such an orientation drives the college's effort to pursue the overarching mission of the college—helping students, regardless of age, interests, career plans, cultural and ethnic background, financial status, or disability, to achieve their goals.

BACKGROUND

   Brookhaven College is one of seven independently accredited comprehensive community colleges within the Dallas County Community College District (DCCCD) (TX). Strategically located within Dallas County, the seven publicly supported colleges provide the 1.9 million county citizens equitable proximity to a community college. Brookhaven College, founded in 1978, is located in the suburban North Dallas city of Farmers Branch. The college's service area is at the center of one of the fastest-growing business communities in the nation.

   Brookhaven College serves approximately 8,000 credit students (2,300 full-time and 5,700 part-time). An additional, 8,000-10,000 students register in noncredit continuing education each semester. Reflecting the communities it serves, Brookhaven College's student population is significantly multicultural. The college serves 2,400 international students representing more than 100 countries and 65 languages. The student population is 69 percent Anglo, 12 percent Hispanic, nine percent African-American, and eight percent Asian. The average age of the student body is 28, with the largest percentage between the ages of 20-24. Notably, the college serves an increasing number of adult seniors.

REFERENCES

Bumphus, W.G. "Quality Initiatives Developed by Colloquium Participants." In Bumphus, W.G. and Johnson, S.L. (eds.), *Continuous Quality Improvement and Student Development: A Partnership for the Future*. Iowa City, IA: The American College Testing Program, 1995, 35-39.

Burke, B. "Continuous Quality Improvement and the Development and Implementation of a Student Registration System." In Bumphus, W.G. and Johnson, S.L. (eds.), *Continuous Quality Improvement and Student Development: A Partnership for the Future*. Iowa City, IA: The American College Testing Program, 1995, 22-26.

Crosby, P. *Philip Crosby's Reflections on Quality*. New York: McGraw-Hill, 1996.

Hammond, B. (District Chair, Texas Workforce Commission). Address to president's cabinet, Brookhaven College, Farmers Branch, Texas, May 30, 1996.

Johnson, S.L. "The Concepts of Continuous Quality Improvement Used in College Faculty and Staff Training." In Bumphus, W.G. and Johnson, S.L. (eds.), *Continuous Quality Improvement and Student Development: A Partnership for the Future*. Iowa City, IA: The American College Testing Program, 1995, 15-17.

Packwood, G. "Issues in Assessing Institutional Effectiveness." In Doucette, D. and Hughes, B. (eds.), *Accessing Institutional Effectiveness in Community Colleges*. Mission Viejo, CA: League for Innovation in the Community College, 1990, 45-49.

Pew Higher Education Roundtable. "Shared Purposes." *Policy Perspectives*, 1996, *6* (4), 1-12.

Seymour, D. *On Q: Causing Quality in Higher Education*. Phoenix, AZ: American Council on Education, Oryx Press, 1993.

Thomas, E.L. "Using Continuous Quality Improvement in Planning and Building a New Student Services Center." In Bumphus, W.G. and Johnson, S.L. (eds.), *Continuous Quality Improvement and Student Development: A Partnership for the Future*. Iowa City, IA: The American College Testing Program, 1995, 18-21.

Chapter VII

Thus far, chapter authors have embraced the critical importance of agreement upon missions and visions; the implementation of inclusionary practices that involve individuals in and out of the college in improving services; and focused, serious attention to the selection of effectiveness indicators, standards, and assessment. These descriptions of progress toward effectiveness goals have been drawn against a backdrop of external pressures not unlike those felt by the overwhelming majority of contemporary colleges. However, the following chapter poignantly describes a unique opportunity for applying the particulars of these broad initiatives in a remarkable story of rebirth—an opportunity that few others have been offered in recent experience.

Jim Tschechtelin, president, Baltimore City Community College (MD), describes how a college can literally begin again, albeit with an awesome responsibility for setting goals, measuring results, training high-performance people, and instilling positive mental attitudes in all members of the college community. His story underscores and puts an extraordinary spin on Ted Marchese's observation: "In my professional lifetime, few issues have vexed the academic world so deeply as accountability does today."[1]

The issues in this chapter focus on radical change, implemented in record time, that continues as a process of examining institutional culture and professional thinking and ethics, working toward improved student retention, evaluating professional performance, and implementing institutionwide measurement strategies. It is less a how-to description than a success story that will offer a new look at the tough issues in the areas of change, performance evaluation, measurement, and money.

[1]Marchese, T. "Accountability." *Change*, November/December 1994, 26, 4.

James D. Tschechtelin
President
Baltimore City Community College
Baltimore, Maryland

THE BALTIMORE PHOENIX

What gets measured gets done.
—Tom Peters

The former Community College of Baltimore (CCB) was pressured by the condition of the city of Baltimore, the condition of the college, and legislative action into dramatic change. A brief story is told here of a college in distress, literally abolished by an act of legislation that was written and passed in the hope that a college might be saved. This story is followed by a fuller narrative that describes that college rising from its own ashes. Policies and programs of the Baltimore phoenix create a compelling picture of effective responses to the unique challenges of re-creation. Moreover, they point the way toward achieving an education mission and, ultimately, earning an acceptable level of public confidence.

The condition of the city of Baltimore. Baltimore, while a city of many loving and talented men and women, has some deeply serious problems. Fifty percent of the AFDC mothers in Maryland live in Baltimore. Of Baltimore's 703,000 residents, 120,000 are on welfare (40,000 women and 80,000 children). Baltimore is in the top four cities nationally in AIDS deaths; AIDS is the leading cause of death for both young men and young women in Baltimore. Baltimore is the third-worst metropolitan area in terms of job growth, behind only Pittsburgh and Philadelphia. Maryland ranks eighth in the nation in the number of prisoners per capita, and one-half of the persons in Maryland prisons come from Baltimore. Fifty-six percent of Baltimore's African-American males aged 18-35 are in the criminal justice system (for example, on probation, awaiting trial, on parole, or in prison). Prevented by law from extending its geographic boundary, the city has a tax base that has been eroded by the migration of wealthier residents to the suburbs. These facts have left their mark on Baltimore schools. Fifty percent of ninth-graders in Baltimore do not graduate from high school. In the 1995 administration of the Maryland School Performance Assessment

Program (MSPAP) for third, fifth, and eighth grades, only 14 percent of the students in Baltimore scored at the satisfactory level or higher, versus a state average of 40 percent. Given the low educational attainment of students, it is not surprising that the 1990 college participation rate (the percentage of Baltimore residents enrolled in any Maryland college or university) was only 0.9 percent, the lowest in the state and less than half the state average rate of 2.18 percent.

The condition of the college. The Community College of Baltimore, founded in 1947, had fallen upon hard times during the 1980s. Enrollment declined by 46 percent during the decade, while enrollment in other Maryland community colleges grew by 22 percent. Student retention and graduation figures were by far the lowest in the state: 24 percent of the new full-time freshmen had graduated, transferred, or were still enrolled four years after entry, compared with a state average of 46 percent. Moreover, financial support from the city of Baltimore had waned, and the college operated at only 75 percent of the state average cost per student. There were recurring material weaknesses in the financial audit. The modest assets of the college foundation were in a noninterest-bearing checking account. The technology of the president's office was a Selectric II typewriter. Relationships between the faculty and administration were contentious; moreover, the faculty refused to nominate one of its own for an outstanding teaching award and financial prize proposed by the board of trustees. While many faculty and staff were dedicated to their tasks and students, some were mired in a negative mental attitude that evolved into a victim mentality. This outlook was characterized by expressions such as, "It's not my fault," "We've had that problem here for a long time," and "They're picking on us."

Legislative action. The problems of Baltimore and the Community College of Baltimore provided significant impetus for change, but a catalyst was needed to make things happen. Into this difficult picture stepped three individuals who saw both the problems of the city and the promise of a strong community college capable of addressing them. In 1989, the Maryland Secretary of Higher Education, Shaila Aery, proposed a radical change to Governor William Donald Schaefer—the life of CCB should be legally ended and a new, state-sponsored college should be created in its place. A highly respected state senator from Baltimore, Clarence Blount, agreed with the need for radical change and joined the effort to create a new institution to replace the existing Community College of Baltimore.

Not everyone concurred with the proposal. Some state policymakers thought that meaningful change at the college was impossible and proposed that the college simply be closed. When the votes were taken, the 1990 legislation created a new college, but it required (1) a plan by which the new college would be developed and (2) a review of the plan by the Maryland

General Assembly in 1992. The legislation included an absolute sunset provision: if the General Assembly did not vote to approve the plan, the college would close in June 1993.

The 1990 legislation was potent. It ended the existence of the Community College of Baltimore and established a new, state-sponsored community college. At midnight on June 30, 1990, the Community College of Baltimore died, and at 12:01 a.m. on July 1, a new institution was born. Among other things, the legislation:

- created a new nine-member board of trustees (including a voting student member), appointed by the governor rather than by the mayor of the City of Baltimore, and specified that the majority of trustees must live in Baltimore
- mandated a thorough review of the mission and curriculum;
- required the evaluation of the performance of all faculty and staff within six months
- assured employment for all employees for only six months
- made a financial commitment to the new college
- provided that all of the assets of the college would become the property of the state and all of the liabilities would remain with the city of Baltimore
- eliminated tenure and collective bargaining for faculty
- removed the college from the state's enrollment-driven community college funding formula and placed it on a "negotiated budget" process like that of the University of Maryland.

These radical moves required the new college to build itself on a foundation of institutional assessment and solid planning. The state's timetable was met; and in 1992, a plan for the new college was developed and submitted to the governor and the Maryland General Assembly. The plan satisfied state leaders who passed the legislation; Baltimore City Community College (BCCC) became a permanent state institution by margins of 107-16 in the House of Delegates and 42-1 in the Senate.

The Process

The process for developing the college's institutional effectiveness model was crafted by five main groups: the governor, the Maryland General Assembly, the Maryland Higher Education Commission, the college's board of trustees, and the President's Council.

The governor and the Maryland General Assembly established an overall structure for the process, set deadlines, and set requirements for a specific 10-part plan to be developed within 16 months. This plan was to include a mission statement; an accountability plan; an assessment of academic programs, personnel and policies; and long-term projections of enrollment, operating costs, and capital needs. A six-month deadline was set for the evaluation of all faculty and staff.

The Maryland Higher Education Commission worked with the college in the development of the plan and reviewed it prior to its submission to the governor and the General Assembly, ensuring that the new college incorporated mechanisms to capture key information about the college as part of the state's higher education data system. Each higher education institution in Maryland annually must submit information about enrollment, the performance of (and remedial courses taken by) recent high school graduates, degrees awarded, transfer students, and full-time employees. Such information enables the Commission to monitor a number of key indicators, including student success (defined by the Commission as the percentage of new full-time students who have graduated, transferred, or are still enrolled four years after entry). The existence of this type of statewide data proved to be a critical element in setting performance goals for the new college and tracking progress toward achieving them. The Commission also requires every public college and university in Maryland to submit an annual Report on Student Learning Outcomes, documenting advancement on key indicators, and, in the case of poor performance on the indicators, plans for improvements.

The college's board of trustees also moved to set the tone for the college. During its first three months, it hired an interim president, approved a revised mission statement, and approved substantive policies regarding curricula and the evaluation of faculty and administrators. The board insisted upon the application of the policies it adopted and was willing to take decisive action. Seven career programs were discontinued in 1991 and 1992. An annual evaluation was implemented for the president and included mutually set goals at the beginning of each academic year; the goals included specific references to key indicators of quality. At their meetings, the trustees received regular reports from the staff about progress on each strategic priority that had been approved by the board.

The board and the President's Council were charged with designing and implementing the college's institutional effectiveness model within the framework for change created by the govenor, the General Assembly, and the Maryland Higher Education Commission. The President's Council met twice a month for policy development and strategic planning. Membership on the council consisted of the president, the vice presidents, the president of the Faculty Senate, a representative from the Student Governance Board, a member of the classified staff, the director of research and planning, the director of public relations, and the assistant attorney general for the college. With the exception of personnel actions, no recommendations were taken to the board without review by the President's Council.

The Institutional Effectiveness Model

The institutional effectiveness model that grew out of these early activities and decisions has similarities to those of other colleges seeking to improve quality, but it is designed to address the unique challenges imposed on the college by the strong mandate to change, by the urban setting, and by a high proportion of academically underprepared students. The BCCC effectiveness model is intended to put forth an overall design for institutional renewal and quality improvement. The model includes four highly interrelated parts (Figure 1).

CLEAR GOALS	MEASUREMENT OF RESULTS
HIGH PERFORMANCE PEOPLE	POSITIVE MENTAL ATTITUDE

Figure 1: Institutional Effectiveness Model

Clear goals. A college wishing to improve must improve toward a specific end. At BCCC, those ends are spelled out in its vision, mission, and goals, including goals for students. The college's vision statement begins:

The vision of the college is to lift the human spirit. Every person dreams of becoming someone special and of doing something extraordinary. The college is a bridge from those dreams to productive employment and to a four-year college. It is a bridge from a factory-based economy to an information- and technology-based economy.

The college's mission is to provide quality, accessible, and affordable education to help develop the full potential and productivity of the citizens of Baltimore. As a state-supported, comprehensive, two-year, degree-granting college, it provides technical and career education, transfer preparation in the arts and sciences, creative continuing education programs for adults and businesses, and developmental education and success strategies, with a mastery of critical thinking skills stressed in each area.

The board emphasized the role that quality would play in the mission of the college. Within the context of the vision and mission (and within 45 days after the college was officially established), the trustees set three key operational goals, which essentially defined what *quality* would mean at Baltimore City Community College:

- BCCC will rank in the top one-third in the state in the student success rate as measured by the percentage of new full-time students who have graduated, transferred, or are still enrolled four years after entry.
- BCCC will rank in the top one-third in the state in full-time employment in the field of training among graduates of career programs.
- BCCC will rank in the top one-third in the state in student transfer goal achievement, as measured by the proportion of graduates who transfer to a four-year college when that was their goal, and by the proportion of transfer students who are in good academic standing at the transfer institution.

At the time that these goals were set, the college ranked a distant last in student success rate, seventh among 17 community colleges in employment in the field of training, and in the bottom one-half in terms of transfer student performance.

The establishment of clear goals included setting high expectations for students. A Covenant for Success promotes explicit discussion of the high expectations that must be in place to promote student success. The document recognizes the mutual responsibilities of faculty and students in the total educational process, and faculty members are asked to make it a part of their introductory material on the first day of class. The covenant is discussed with students in a two-day orientation program and published in the college catalog.

At Baltimore City Community College, we believe that the seeds of greatness are in each student. It is through education that the gifts and talents in each student are realized. Faculty, staff, and students have complementary and mutual responsibilities to assure student success. The purpose of this covenant for success is to describe those mutual responsibilities.

COVENANT FOR SUCCESS
As a faculty or staff member of Baltimore City Community College:

- I will have high expectations for each student. I will not accept mediocrity.
- I will encourage each student to become all that he or she is capable of becoming.
- I will value time, start and end classes on time, and set priorities for the use of time.
- I will be enthusiastic about my work. I will go out of my way to stay current in my field and find creative ways to teach my subject in a manner that is interesting and relevant to students.
- I will respect students and value their immense potential. I will not label students or place limitations on them about goals that they are willing to work hard to achieve.

- I will respect differences among students and encourage students to learn from their differences.

As a student at Baltimore City Community College:

- I am responsible for my education. While others may help me, my success will depend primarily upon what I do to become successful. If it is to be, it is up to me.
- I will work hard to succeed. This includes attending all classes and devoting a great deal of time to reading, studying, and doing out-of-class assignments. I will spend at least two hours in outside preparation for each hour of class time.
- I will value time, come to classes on time, and set priorities for the use of time.
- I will set positive, specific, and measurable goals; and I will visualize myself in possession of them.
- I will be an active learner. I will ask questions and seek help as often as needed.
- I will be honest and maintain the highest level of integrity.

Measurement of results. The establishment of clear goals had set the stage for measurement of results. The "bottom line" at BCCC is measured with the three key indicators, defined by the board: student retention/graduation, graduate employment rate, and transfer achievement. The college's Office of Institutional Research provides robust support for the measurement of results, publishing several reports each year that help to display key results. One of these reports is the *Data Book*, which includes information about enrollment, placement test results, course pass rates, student retention rates, employment and transfer outcomes, degrees awarded, employees, finances, and facilities. Another publication of the Office of Institutional Research is the *Report on Student Learning Outcomes*, required by the Maryland Higher Education Commission and including sections about student success, employment and transfer outcomes, and continuing education.

High-performance people. A college can have clear goals and can measure results against those goals, but without talented men and women to teach and operate the institution, its goals will never be achieved. The term "high-performance people" is defined as trustees, faculty, and staff who are exceptionally skilled, ethical, and industrious.

In establishing BCCC, the Maryland General Assembly stipulated that a new board of trustees would be appointed by the governor, rather than the previous system of appointment by the mayor of Baltimore. The governor selected an entirely new board and met with members in a private session to communicate his expectations for quality and change. The BCCC trustees developed a clear sense of their roles. They asked the staff tough questions, and in particular, focused on three important questions: "Where are we going?" (mission), "How will we get there?" (programs), and "How are we doing?" (results). The trustees focused on policy development and broad direction of the college, leaving the administration and the implementation of policy to the staff; but they did their homework, coming to board meetings prepared to dig into the agenda.

Students spend more time with faculty than with any other group at the college. The methods used to develop a high-performance faculty included a rigorous evaluation system, a strong program of affirmation for outstanding work, and extensive involvement in the college governance process. Under a mandate from the Maryland General Assembly, the college evaluated all full-time faculty in the fall 1990 semester. The faculty evaluation system included: (1) student ratings of the faculty, (2) peer evaluations, (3) an unannounced classroom visit by the department chair, and (4) an overall rating by the department chair. (Student ratings were conducted using the Student Instructional Report [SIR], published by the Educational Testing Service. Grounded in extensive research, the SIR has three factor scores to describe student ratings: organization, faculty-student interaction, and communica-tion.) Using the four sources of data, the vice president rated each faculty member as excellent, good, fair, or poor.

In an effort to affirm the work of outstanding faculty, the board estab-lished College Excellence Awards. These awards are based upon written nominations, and recipients are selected by a committee of faculty and staff who have received the award in previous years. The award is given to two full-time and two part-time faculty each year at meetings of the board of trustees. Their names are inscribed on a collective plaque, and they each receive a certificate and a $500 honorarium. Full-time faculty members who receive the College Excellence Awards also receive funds to attend the annu-al International Conference on Teaching and Leadership Excellence, hosted by the National Institute for Staff and Organizational Development (NISOD) each May. In addition to these formal recognitions, the president also presents Celebration of Achievement Awards—informal certificates given at the three collegewide meetings during the academic year. In six years, 547 Celebration of Achievement Awards have been given to faculty, administrators, and pro-fessional and support staff members.

The faculty are involved in all aspects of the college and participate in a wide variety of committees. The president of the faculty senate is a member of the President's Council (the primary body that develops policy recom-mendations to the board of trustees); meets every two weeks with the college president; and has a regular place on the agenda of the monthly meeting of the board of trustees.

The development of high-performance administrators and professional staff at BCCC follows the same path as the development of such faculty: evaluation, affirmation, and involvement. College Excellence Awards are given annually by the board of trustees to two administrators or professional staff members and to two members of the classified staff. Celebration of Achievement Awards are presented regularly to outstanding administrators and professional staff.

Positive mental attitude. The presence of clear goals and the measurement of results by high-performance people do not lead to success without a strong and abiding positive mental attitude. At BCCC, a positive mental attitude is described as a pattern of thought that dwells more on possibilities than on problems. It is a belief that change is possible; it is a sense of confident expectancy that says "can do" rather than "cannot." The concept of the positive mental attitude is based upon twin assumptions: (1) people can choose their outlook on life and are free to decide whether the outlook will be positive or negative, and (2) people who achieve are people who think they can achieve. This phenomenon has been called the law of expectancy.

A positive mental attitude is an important counterweight for the meaninglessness and hopelessness that many see in their communities. Creating a positive mental attitude in students begins with the faculty and staff; however, early on, some at the college believed that a turnaround was impossible. One faculty member remarked, after looking at statewide data on student success in relation to local economic conditions, that the likelihood of change at BCCC was almost hopeless: "Unless you change the economy of Baltimore, you can't change the student success rate." This attitude must not become a self-fulfilling prophecy; if a college is to improve its effectiveness, there must be an abiding belief that positive change is possible.

Positive mental attitudes have been taught at BCCC by example and encouragement, by teaching the concept, and through staff selection. The positive actions of leaders in the college, especially in difficult situations, have set a tone that was learned by others. The college's extensive program of awards and affirmations have provided important encouragement. The theory and applications of a positive philosophy have been presented and discussed at staff meetings and at faculty convocations; motivational speakers have addressed students and staff. A positive mental attitude has been taught in a new course—the College Success Seminar; two-day workshops have educated faculty about the course. And, finally, positive people have been sought out to fill the vacancies in faculty and staff positions.

Lessons Learned and Conclusions

The phoenix is a mythical bird that is said to have risen from its own ashes. The Community College of Baltimore was in deep trouble with enrollment, finances, management, and image. The state of Maryland took a bold and unusual step to end the life of one college and create another. With the vision and determination of many talented people, a new college has risen. The past six years have been a roller coaster of motion and emotion. Along the way, numerous lessons were learned that can be applied in other colleges grappling with the tough issues in the areas of change, performance evaluation, measurement, and money.

In order to make a significant change in student retention, it must be a conscious and consistently high institutional priority. The board of trustees, administrators, and faculty must be committed to creating and implementing policies and programs that will make a difference. Many competing interests on a college campus vie for attention—personnel problems, budget shortfalls, and political intrigues. Moreover, student retention is not a naturally alluring topic to the news media, which more often will choose to write stories about enrollment or finances.

There is a paradox in radical change: You must involve people, but you can't involve them! Lasting change depends upon the participation of the persons who will be affected. But as the numbers of individuals involved in decision making increase, the less likely it is that major change will be effected. Each time the circle widens, more groups and subgroups present their interests, and a unifying, single vision is more difficult to create. Some tension and anxiety must and will occur if substantive changes are to take place, and the leadership challenge is to seek a judicious balance between wide involvement and centrally stimulated action.

Vast problems demand vast solutions. Those in charge cannot tinker with a major problem and have any realistic chance of creating a lasting improvement. The Community College of Baltimore was a deeply troubled college. An intervention on one or two dimensions, such as simply replacing the tenure system or appointing a new board of trustees, would not have been sufficient to turn the institution around. A comprehensive approach needed to be applied to the changes that were needed; and all areas of the college were affected, including governance, administration, curriculum, personnel, policies, and finance.

There must be consequences for poor performance. It is significant that the Maryland General Assembly included a clear repercussion for nonperformance. The statute under which the college began in 1990 included an absolute sunset provision: If the plan presented for the future of the institution was unacceptable, the college was to be closed. This had a dramatic effect upon the development of the new college and its policies. The presence of this "hammer" made it clear that change was expected. In the internal deliberations about new policies, the discussion often boiled down to such questions as, "What's wrong with what we are doing now?" "Why can't we leave this like it is?" In these situations, it was possible to remind participants that if the

General Assembly did not want serious change, they never would have passed the legislation.

Changing the institutional culture is at the root of significant change, and changing the culture of a college takes time. There is still a long way to go at Baltimore City Community College. The culture was shaped and formed over many years and has not yielded to quick revision. Student retention continues to be far below what it should be, and daily frustrations are still present. While most faculty and staff go the extra mile every day to help make impressive gains possible, not everyone at the college is "on board" in terms of commitment. Some faculty and staff members see institutional effectiveness as an important issue, but not as "my problem" to address. Having a Covenant for Success, for example, does not guarantee that every faculty member knows about it, believes in it, and discusses it with his or her students.

A strong, unified, policy-oriented, and supportive board of trustees has been essential to progress. It is axiomatic that a board sets the policy for a college, but even more important that it sets the tone. It has been important for persons inside and outside of the college to know that the board will insist on fairness as well as accountability and that its job is policy and not administration. Such a board expects the president to run the day-to-day operation of the college and resists the temptation to micro-manage. For example, when a board of trustees understands the importance of retention and provides the president with the support to make the changes necessary to attack attrition, the president is well-armed for the battles that often occur en route to the solution. Without that support, the president will be hard-pressed to make meaningful change.

Performance evaluation of faculty and staff has been perhaps the most difficult single task at the college. Franklin P. Jones said, "Honest criticism is hard to take, particularly from a relative, a friend, an acquaintance, or a stranger" (McWilliams, 1995, p. 152). Jones' humor reveals great truth. When people are asked, "Would you like feedback about how to improve in your work?" or "Are there areas for potential growth?" nearly everyone says, "Yes." Yet, when constructive feedback is given, most persons struggle to accept it in a positive way. The evaluation of faculty has been especially difficult. The use of the Student Instructional Report (SIR) as part of the evaluation process has been a major point of contention with many faculty members. Some faculty members say that students in developmental courses cannot read the survey well enough to respond accurately; others believe that undue reliance is placed on student ratings, and others remark that the SIR is a popularity contest.

Over the years, the faculty evaluation process has been revised somewhat with input and assistance from a committee of faculty members. Peer evaluation as a part of a summative evaluation has been discontinued; faculty ratings of each other were so compressed at the excellent end of the scale as to render them practically useless in making distinctions about the range of quality. As a result, the process was adapted to incorporate faculty goals. At the beginning of every academic year, each faculty member develops goals for the year in consultation with the department chair. Department chairs currently evaluate faculty members based upon the faculty member's goal achievement, the faculty member's self-assessment, an unannounced class-room visit, and student evaluations.

The last resort when coaching a faculty or staff member toward improve-ment is termination, a painful and difficult process. There is very little short-term gain from taking a tough stand against ineffective faculty and staff mem-bers. It is frustrating, time-consuming, and distressing to all concerned. For these reasons, most managers simply do not think it is worth their effort. In the long term, however, rigorous performance evaluation of faculty and staff is an absolutely necessary condition to excellence and an effective institution.

There is a certain "measaphobia" in higher education, and it works against true progress. Some people fear an emphasis on the measurement of outcomes. The key is not to measure everything, but to find meaningful mea-sures of key indicators of performance and to properly interpret and use the data. All colleges begin with a vision, but that vision cannot be translated into reality unless the college keeps track of progress—that is, unless the college measures results.

One struggle in the measurement of results is between the organization-al need for objectivity and the human need for self-satisfaction. On the one hand, if a program is not achieving its intended purpose, there should be valid and reliable data that clearly indicate that condition. On the other hand, there is a human temptation to find positive variables and data (or to dismiss data) to "look good." This dilemma exists at all levels and is apparent in the following examples:

- What does it mean if the student ratings of a faculty member are "good" according to the rating scale on the survey form but are in the bottom 10 percent among all student ratings of faculty members at the college? Does it mean that the faculty member is teaching in a dif-ficult discipline? Does it mean that the faculty member should not receive a good evaluation from the department chair?
- What does it mean if the graduate employment rate in an accounting program is low and declining? Does it mean that the program should be redesigned? Does it mean that the job market for accounting degrees is changing?
- What does it mean if the retention-to-graduation rate is lower for an urban community college than a community college in a wealthy suburban county? Does it mean that the urban community college is lower in quality? Does it mean that the urban college should receive more (or less) government support?

These are examples of the difficult questions that are asked inevitably when results are measured; they can cause disdain and fear. However, the measurement of results has been instrumental to progress at BCCC. We have discovered that the solution to fears about measurement lies not in evading the issue, but in systematically and specifically defining goals, and then asking how we will know when we have reached them.

Money is probably overrated by educators as a solution to problems in community colleges. This heretical sentence needs an explanation. The commitment for increased state aid to BCCC has not yet been realized because of the impact of the recession on the Maryland economy. Although state funds have been generously provided for capital projects, state aid for operating expenditures is actually lower today than when the college became a state institution.

And while some faculty and staff would point to lack of funding as the number one problem of the institution, their analysis is incorrect. Lack of money is often used as an excuse to avoid tackling other serious problems, such as poor teamwork, loose performance evaluation, and administrative inefficiencies. For example, in the early days of BCCC, some faculty said, "Yes, I haven't been too productive, but that's because the administration did not reward additional effort." Some of the administrators responded, "We never had enough money to keep the faculty happy." This type of reciprocal blaming consumed the psychological energy of the college, leaving less energy to focus on solvable problems. This is certainly not to say that money is unimportant. Money is important, but the lack of it should not serve as an excuse for ignoring serious problems that are within a college's control.

The most important and overarching lesson learned is that, even in a situation where times are tough and the outlook bleak, **substantive change in the quality of a community college is possible**. With the proper mixture of clear goals, the measurement of results, high-performance people, and a positive mental attitude, the dreams of students can be realized through our work. H.G. Wells's observation that human history is a race between education and catastrophe is being played out dramatically in many of our cities—and, in many, catastrophe appears to be winning. Strong and effective community colleges, however, are capable of evening the odds that education and students will be the winners.

BACKGROUND

Maryland's residents enjoy mountains in the west, ocean beaches in the east, and urban and suburban life in between. With about five million residents living in 24 political subdivisions, Maryland ranks 19th in U.S. population; 31 percent of the residents are minorities, primarily African-Americans. The state ranks high in the educational attainment of its citizens; 27 percent of its residents age 25 and above have at least a four-year degree. With a highly educated workforce, its per capita income ranks fifth in the nation.

Nestled by the Chesapeake Bay, Baltimore is a beautiful city of 92 square miles and 703,000 people. It is city of rich history and poor people. Famous for its shipbuilding and rail transportation, Baltimore was for many years a magnet for people with a dream. Men and women came to the city for its plentiful jobs and abundant opportunities. Times changed, though, and manufacturing plants either closed or moved to the suburbs. While the Inner Harbor now attracts millions of visitors and the life sciences are becoming the engine of economic development, the challenges that accompany poverty are easy to see in Baltimore. Baltimore surpasses all of the counties in the state in the percentage of persons living in poverty, and it ranks third in unemployment rate.

In 1995, the Baltimore City Community College (BCCC) enrolled 5,970 credit and 7,361 noncredit students on two campuses. The college offers 22 career and six transfer programs, as well as a noncredit focus on customized training, literacy, and continuing professional education. BCCC students are friendly and degree-oriented; 81 percent of the students are seeking an associate's degree or a certificate. Eighty-five percent of the students are Baltimore residents. Among credit students, 75 percent are female, 67 percent are part-time, and 82 percent are African-American; the average age is 30. Fifty-nine percent of the students have a household income below $20,000 per year; 78 percent are single, widowed, or divorced; and 48 percent have one or more dependents. About 58 percent of the students receive some financial aid. Eighty-five percent of the entering students are placed in at least one developmental course, and the pass rates in developmental courses range from 41 to 63 percent. There are 404 full-time employees, including 117 full-time faculty.

REFERENCES

McWilliams, P. *The Portable Life 101*. Los Angeles: Prelude Press, 1995.

Chapter VIII

From the story of a college driven by legislative mandate toward radical change, we turn to a story of a college driven by its own analysis of the future effects of reduced resources and other external pressures. Robert Gordon, president of Humber College of Applied Arts and Technology (CN), describes the new beginnings that the college initiated during the deep recession of the early 1980s. An Academic Council was created as a conduit to involvement and as a body for directional advice. Clearly, the traditionally informal incorporation of the values of risk-taking, innovation, and excellence had to be formalized if the college was to maintain its significant strength. The Council was to serve as a mechanism for substantiating effectiveness and fostering cooperation and resource sharing.

As have other chapter authors, Gordon describes the significance of reformulating the mission statement and recasting or refocusing the vision of where the college ought to be going in light of external circumstances and pressures. Key indicators of success were drawn from this new interpretation of the organization culture and values, and now drive the process of transformation. Humber analyzes the unique perspectives of the wide diversity of stakeholder groups and measures its effectiveness according to how well it serves these diverse constituencies. Information-handling, collecting, processing, reporting, and interpreting effectiveness measurement data are currently approaching "taken-for-granteds" in the institution. As other contributors have observed, the use of continuous review and assessment, cross-functional teams, and steering committees are critical to energizing and implementing new challenges and opportunities.

Robert A. Gordon
President
Humber College of Applied Arts and Technology
Toronto, Ontario, Canada

SEEKING QUALITY AT HUMBER COLLEGE THROUGH A PROCESS FOR TRANSFORMATION

The real voyage of discovery consists not in
seeking new landscapes but in having new eyes.
—Marcel Proust

Processes to hold Ontario colleges accountable for their effectiveness are in a state of evolution. The colleges, as institutions, are not accredited by an external, central body or agency. However, a special provincial government agency, known as the College Standards and Accreditation Council (CSAC), was recently created as a result of a major study of the Ontario colleges (Council of Regents) to begin a process for establishing common program standards (learning outcomes) and guidelines for a program accreditation framework. It is proposed that diploma and post-diploma programs would be accredited on an individual basis using general criteria such as student evaluation, record systems, learning resources, and opportunities, and that these could be incorporated into the systems each college already has for ensuring its graduates meet program standards (CSAC, 1996). Be that as it may, it is too early to judge the impact of CSAC's endeavor with program standards—only seven sets (out of a total of 400 programs) have been developed at this time—although some Humber College personnel are concerned that the effort will tend to produce standards that are lower than those presently in place. The provincial program-accreditation framework and its implementation guidelines have become matters of concern, even controversy, as Humber continues to develop and improve its own program quality process.

At Humber, quality is an internal college responsibility that means doing what we say we will do, on time, every time—ideally, exceeding the expectations of stakeholders. Effectiveness involves the continuous process of ensuring that the college is achieving its stated mission and goals. At Humber, this process is a collective staff responsibility led by senior management. Continuous quality improvement (CQI) is an outcome of the transformational human resource development process currently in place.

The college mission states the critical success factors and quantitative and qualitative measures of the indicators of those factors are proposed, developed, tested, and implemented incrementally and collectively. In the case of Humber, the process is intentionally "organic" and has evolved in a context of changing initiatives, trends, and forces impacting the college's pursuit of its mission.

The financial crunch. Shaping the financial context for Humber is the paramount political and economic fact of very large national and provincial debts and continuing annual deficits. The college receives about 60 percent of its operating revenue as a grant from the provincial government, one-half of which is via transfer payments from the federal government. The other 40 percent of operating revenue is generated by student fees (which are fixed by the government); conditional or specific grants; and college-controlled, revenue-generating services. The current provincial government has imposed an overall 14 percent cut for fiscal 1996-97 on the operating revenue and conditional grants to all colleges. As a result, there have been hundreds of layoffs throughout the system, including some 60 at Humber. Attrition and early retirements among the staffs of Ontario colleges have further reduced the numbers. Effectiveness at Humber emerges through the process of developing human capital; thus, strategies for maintaining the pool of expertise and experience either will have to be reinforced or newly developed.

The demand-versus-resources dilemma. The opening up of free trade through the North American Free Trade Agreement (NAFTA), the growing global economy, and the explosion of information and manufacturing technologies, such as the Internet, the electronic highway, robotics, and computer integrated manufacturing (CIM) are fostering a high demand for advanced training or retraining. Toronto is located in the heart of Ontario's high-technology communications and manufacturing industries. The higher expectations, increasing demand, and shrinking resources have placed a stressful burden on the college. Positioning Humber to be able to respond to these demands of its customers has had significant implications for effectiveness.

The changing nature of work. As the global economy develops, new competencies in information technology and strategies in cooperation are needed by today's information workers. These factors cannot be ignored when considering the effectiveness of the contemporary college curriculum (Gordon, 1995a). In addition to vocation-specific competencies required for entry into a chosen field, today's workers and professionals need to be literate in information technology, able to work and solve problems cooperatively, and above all else able to learn in a self-directed and efficient way.

A set of generic, transferable, employability skills has been identified by college working groups and is being integrated into the curriculum. These skills read like a generic job description: communications, numeracy, technological (computer) and information literacy, teamwork and interpersonal relations, analytical thinking, creative thinking, taking responsibility, and learning how to learn. The college is now challenged to develop measures of effectiveness for student success in terms of these generic skills.

Learning-centered education. In 1994, the Royal Commission on Learning published a report recommending a clear direction and vision for Ontario's primary and secondary education systems, including how these components should articulate with postsecondary education. It is significant to note that the Commission identified four fundamental "educational engines" or drivers within the educational milieu: 1) professional development; 2) the formation of alliances or partnerships; 3) student preparation or remediation; and of primary importance, 4) the integration of information technology into the curriculum as a stimulus to learning-centered education. Humber's recently recast mission statement reflects all of these influences.

Strengthening the growing learner-centered ethos is a recent, influential statement for Ontario colleges, commissioned by the Council of Presidents (Academic Vice Presidents, 1995). The presidents perceive a paradigm shift in educational design from a teaching-centered toward a learning-centered approach. The core of the learning-centered approach or learning paradigm is based on learning outcomes (Barr and Tagg, 1995). Learning-centered education calls for the learner to demonstrate outcomes rather than recall facts, processes, and theories. In this approach (which to some college faculty and staff is a new departure), the environment, materials, and resources to assist the learner in acquiring these outcomes are made available on a just-in-time basis. The role of the teacher is critical for developing and implementing the strategies of modularization, mastery of outcomes, self-pacing, and flexible start and finish times. Transformation to this paradigm will affect and change many traditional systems, processes, procedures, roles, and responsibilities (Office of Research and Planning, 1996). As the role of the teacher gradually shifts, the indicators and measures of effectiveness will focus on learning outcomes rather than inputs. Funding could be based on measures of learner-competency or exit skills as an indicator of effectiveness rather than being based on the number of students in a particular program at a particular time to measure student throughput. (This illustration will be expanded further in the last section of this chapter.)

Information technology. Information technology is becoming "taken for granted" in the global work environment, emerging from what is now called the "new economy." With the applications of technology becoming broader and more affordable, the demand for different instructional delivery capabilities is rising and perceived as increasingly vital. A home- or office-based workstation, for example, can allow students to access courses from their home via World Wide Web home pages (Information Technology Task Force, 1995). The variety of the alternative modes of delivery offered by the college is one measure of its flexibility and highlights the need for an evaluation framework to measure and compare the individual effectiveness of these modes.

Diversity. The student body of Humber College is a microcosm of the Toronto population. Presently, Toronto's population is about 40 percent Caucasian with the 60 percent majority consisting of a wide variety of other races constituting approximately 120 distinct ethnic communities and more than 85 spoken languages. Over 40 different language groups are represented among the students at Humber. Nearly half of the 260,000 annual immigrants to Canada settle in the Toronto area; many immediately look to the colleges for further education and language training. Humber is under continuous pressure to meet the challenges of multiethnic, multilinguistic diversity.

In addition to the increasing number of older full- and part-time students (reflecting the increasing average age of the general population and the interest in continuing education), nearly one-fifth of Humber's full-time student population consists of either university graduates or students having some university credits. These students are seeking practical skills for increased employment opportunities. The needs and issues of all of these older students—as compared to younger, direct secondary-school entrants— are expanding the support services the college must offer to respond effectively. The challenges posed by diversity at Humber are many and constitute a corresponding challenge in defining effectiveness in terms of student success.

The underprepared student. Diversity also applies to diverse educational backgrounds and levels of skills and knowledge for entering students. Entry into an Ontario college is legally open to anyone possessing an Ontario Secondary School Diploma (30 credits usually obtained by the end of grade 12), possessing its equivalent, or having mature-student status (19 years or older). There are no provincial, secondary school, or standard learning outcomes; hence, qualified students may vary considerably in their academic performance levels. This variation among provincial school boards and extra provincial standards (learning outcomes) constitutes a major problem for the college in terms of determining entry skills, particularly in communications and mathematics. Extensive testing and remediation are required in order to comply with the legislation regarding accessibility. At Humber, effectiveness with respect to student success is linked with accessibility and the college's ability to deal with diversity in language capability, age, experience, and academic entry-level skills.

All of these political, economic, technological and social initiatives, trends, and forces help to shape Humber College's current approach to effectiveness.

A Transformational Process: The Beginning

The process is the product. Humber adopted a transformational outlook starting in the early 1980s; at the same time, a set of corporate values grew out of and simultaneously supported this emerging outlook. The result has been that the process and the product of Humber's approach to institutional effectiveness are, in effect, one and the same. Being a process, the approach is continuously and strategically evolving. Figure 1 illustrates Humber's dynamic approach to effectiveness.

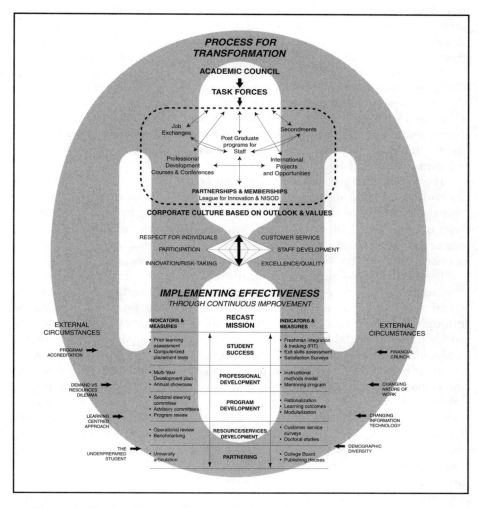

Figure 1: Humber College Process for Transformation and its Outcome—Implementing Effectiveness

The graphic imposes a static, two-dimensional structure on the process for implementing effectiveness through transformation as one way to represent what has happened over the last decade; but, actually, a number of activities and endeavors occurred and are occurring simultaneously, creating dynamism and synergism that have been described as organic. A continuous or "rolling" planning framework is updated annually, and as needed, by working groups drawing on broad input from the stakeholders and is used as a guide to new initiatives. In fact, the leadership approach at Humber during the last decade has been to support and encourage a multitude of initiatives and innovations while providing direction through constantly emerging strategies supporting the mission. This organic, multifaceted approach to development and effectiveness has been Humber's strength and at the same time a continuing challenge in terms of focussing its energies and resources.

As shown in Figure 1 (superimposed on the corporate logo of Humber College), the Academic Council oversees an evolving process of transforming the human potential of the staff. The explicit values of the college, seen in the figure as a "value diamond," act as a central focus; the college's mission flows from these corporate values. The staff have gradually acquired a state of self-motivation and readiness that is helping them to ensure proactively that the mission is accomplished.

The four primary corporate values can be characterized as: 1) respect for individuals as reinforced by customer service, 2) participation, 3) staff development, and 4) innovation and risk-taking incorporating excellence, including high quality. This "value diamond" is promoted by and manifested through senior management support of such activities as contract training, consulting services, international projects, and a staff recognition and awards program.

The effectiveness-generating transformational outlook supported by the "value diamond" is a continuous change process of creating and sustaining social relations, positive attitudes, and a sense of pride, loyalty, and readiness through deliberate strategies to generate involvement, new understandings, and action. The social relations and skills fostered in a participatory climate create at Humber a state of readiness for change—a "critical mass" of human resource potential. This organizational energy requires nurturing; but after more than a decade of purposeful and incremental development, it is now capable of regeneration and self-renewal. Evidence of this regenerative power lies in the output and outcomes of a Humber "Moving Forward" conference and workshop attended by over 200 staff members working in 18 teams for three days in spring 1995. A strategic framework for planning improvement goals and objectives over the next three years was designed and action plans developed. The transformational process emanating from the outlook to deliberately promote this critical level of readiness has been ongoing since the landmark governance shift to an Academic Council initiated in the 1980s.

New beginnings. The founding president's leadership style was actualized through a management team approach with each academic division of the college organized around a reasonably independent dean. The college was relatively well resourced in the early period from 1967 to the late 1970s. A compromise strategy worked well during this time, for the president commanded respect and was known for his humanitarian, personalizing qualities. The independence of the academic divisions and the adequate funding base permitted experimentation, rapid-growth initiatives, and ventures which drew on the creativity and talent of the faculty and administrators. Although there were many committees and meetings, major decisions were usually made in camera by the senior management team; their negotiating and compromise-making skills maintained the momentum of the college.

The early 1980s was a time of comparatively deep recession, and it was apparent that compromise and negotiation among reasonably independent academic divisions in an environment of scarce resources would not maintain the strength of the organization nor lay the necessary foundations for the future. A different leadership style and approach for a reduced-resource organization would be needed to foster participation and preparedness.

Creating the Academic Council. The incoming president created an advisory Academic Council loosely analogous to a university senate. This elected council was formed to represent broadly all constituencies and major units within the college. The group was intended primarily as a conduit to involvement and solid directional advice rather than as a "super planning" or policymaking committee.

The culture of the college already incorporated the values of risk-taking, innovation, and excellence on an informal basis and demonstrated a competitive propensity between and among divisions and units. This competition had increased to what some would call "turf wars" in the early 1980s as funding was steadily reduced. An organizational development intervention such as the Academic Council was seen as a mechanism to substantiate effectiveness and to foster greater cooperation and resource sharing. At the same time, the existing informal risk-taking approach was encouraged through numerous business ventures, including the provision of training services, trading land for buildings, and exchanging the use of space for access to the latest technology.

Transformation as the genesis of effectiveness. The creation of the Academic Council signalled a paradigm shift towards globalizing input, empowering stakeholders, and reallocating resources more toward support for learners. The Academic Council's legitimacy for identifying issues, and investigating and making recommendations regarding these issues laid the foundation of the process for transformation by providing opportunities and stimuli for cross-functional and multitasked participation and development of staff through task forces, as indicated at the top of Figure 1.

Committees and task forces were initiated by the president over the next decade (14, so far) to deal with effectiveness issues such as program review, the college mission, remediation for underprepared students, the evaluation of faculty, developmental issues such as multiculturalism, violence and safety in the college, and a code of ethics for students and staff. More recent task force endeavors include the marketing of programs and services, and information technology and its impact on learning. These broad-based task force activities promote collegewide involvement and buy-in, as well as create and enhance social relations, cooperation, and resource-sharing.

Other reinforcing and enhancing transformational practices were also initiated as indicated in the dashed box of Figure 1. A comprehensive professional development program and links and partnerships with other institutions and associations, such as the League for Innovation in the Community College and the National Institute for Staff and Organizational Development (NISOD), were established. In addition, many staff have taken advantage of undergraduate and graduate programs specially arranged on-site by the college through Canadian and American universities.

An annually implemented strategy of incremental restructuring involved job exchanges—that is, shifting people among different areas to expose them to new challenges and broaden their experiences. This set of moves and changes in responsibility was carefully considered as a strategy to develop people and to revitalize and make improvements in structures, systems, and processes. It is interesting to note that when the major reengineering of 1994 took place to reorganize four academic divisions into 12 sectoral schools, the process was relatively smooth for an organization the size of Humber.

A complementary practice of seconding (temporarily moving personnel from one position or role to another) and encouraging staff to engage in interim assignments provides a multitude of developmental (for example, transformational) opportunities. The International Projects Office is an exemplar of the process of transformation operating with one full-time, seconded—temporarily assigned—chair, a part-time consultant, and a part-time support person. The plethora of international activity at Humber is handled mainly through full-time staff who take on international projects and consulting in addition to their normal workload. These cross-cultural opportunities and communication experiences help faculty and administrators transform their professional and personal competencies to more effectively meet the needs of the multicultural, multilanguage population within the college.

Effectiveness: The Outcome of the Process for Transformation

Identifying the key indicators of effectiveness. The recent reformulating of the mission statement was a participatory effort in expressing what was already embedded in the culture of the college, integrating this with the vision of where the college ought to be going in the light of external circumstances. This new interpretation of the organizational culture and values identifies the critical success factors upon which the energy of the process of transformation is and will be focused as indicated in the bottom half of Figure 1. The four institutional success factors are: 1) student success [the primary factor supported by the three following operational factors]; 2) staff development, including faculty ability to provide flexible delivery of instruction; 3) curriculum with generic skills and general education components to enhance total development and capability, and programs designed to achieve international recognition; and 4) institutional resources, services, and processes. These four aspects of the mission are bolstered by creating alliances and partnerships positioning the college in the community, region, country, and globe.

Each of the above factors is an aspect of the success of the college and, in fact, reflects the developing initiatives, trends, and forces previously outlined. The work of the Academic Council, its complementary activities, the recent "Moving Forward" conference, as well as the ongoing initiatives of the "transformed" staff, constitute the basis for implementing effectiveness through continuous improvement in relation to the success factors and their indicators that are articulated through the college mission statement. Indicators of effectiveness, once identified, must be measured; and decisions and action to make changes and improvements must be made and taken based on the results of those measures.

The primary indicator of effectiveness: Student success. For student success, the major indicator of effectiveness is achievement of learning outcomes. The college has been working formally for the past three years on identifying outcomes in each program and anticipates completing the task in 1997. Additional indicators that reflect student success include student retention, job placement, career status five years after graduation, and satisfaction with the learning experience at Humber College. (Other student- and program-related indicators are included in the final section of this chapter.)

With the shifting orientation toward the learner-centered approach and the need for graduates to acquire not only the vocational skills and knowledge—identified as program learning outcomes—but also broader, transferable generic skills and general education components, the emphasis in assessment (measurement) is on performance and competence. Students must practice current skills, apply mastered ideas in new ways, and engage others in creating new solutions to new problems by carrying their learning to new limits. Humber is rapidly expanding field experience, team casework, and major projects which are planned to be evaluated by an external panel of experts as the bases of assessment. These external verifiers should provide a measure of the effectiveness of learning so that reviews and decisions regarding instructional methods, learning outcomes, learning services and resources, and faculty competence can be made.

Student entry competencies and retention. Student success is closely linked with student retention. With the emphasis on the student rather than on the institution, a knowledge of the competencies and profiles of the incoming students is critical to planning remediation for the underprepared and the kinds of services needed for interventions aimed at minimizing student dropout rates. Mature students often bring skills and experience directly applicable to their chosen programs. A formal Prior Learning Assessment process has been established at Humber (and throughout the Ontario college system) as a response to the needs of the many mature students of diverse backgrounds applying to the college. These students may challenge learning outcomes and, if successful, be given credit for up to 75 percent of the requisite outcomes, saving time and resources for both the student and the college.

After many years of piloting, the college has adapted The College Board's Computerized Placement Test (CPT) of communications competencies as a requisite for success across the diploma programs. This test is now mandatory for every entering student. Where appropriate, mathematics skills are also tested in the same way. A template for each program allows potential students (primarily high school students who intend to go to college) to take the communications and mathematics tests and to be able to work with the high school (and to take some personal responsibility) to improve their own entry-level competencies in these two areas.

Research which was originally part of one faculty member's doctoral study was recognized as significant for student retention and given corporate support. From an initial dropout rate of 30 percent in selected programs, the resulting intervention over a five-year period has reduced the rate to 15 percent in those same programs. Currently a formal profile-building process for freshmen provides indicators of where individual students may experience difficulty. This Freshmen Integration and Tracking (FIT) system identifies high-risk students so that intervention can be made to increase their probability of success. The incoming student's background and entry characteristics are assessed. At midsemester of their first year, students are given a Student Satisfaction Questionnaire. Also at midsemester, and at subsequent assessment points, the students' evaluation and progress data are compiled in a uniquely designed software program, along with the background and satisfaction data.

The reports and graphs from the FIT "Partners in Education Inventory" package provide feedback to students, counselors, academic advisors, and the school heads for developing prescriptions. This initiative empowers teams of faculty to enhance the quality and timeliness of student advising and improves retention. The student performance information is used annually to refine admissions criteria, marketing literature, and orientation programs. All nonconfidential information is shared with the college to improve the relevance of services and with secondary school partners to improve the preparation of college applicants and the school-to-college transition. This sophisticated tool to improve student persistence will be applied collegewide in the 1996-97 academic year and is being marketed to meet the demands of other colleges as awareness of its success spreads.

In addition, for students well into their programs, an array of support services and alternative learning opportunities is essential to maintaining progress and ensuring success. At Humber, these include peer tutoring, study skills workshops, and open learning centres for communications, mathematics, accounting, and computer applications.

Professional development. Faculty are recruited primarily on the basis of their academic credentials and their direct experience in the field they intend to teach. Like all Ontario colleges, Humber ensures that in-service teacher training is provided during a mandatory two-year probationary period before a faculty member becomes permanent staff. The major effectiveness indicator of the critical success factor of professional development centres on the continued upgrading of faculty, support staff, and administrators. Effectiveness indicators for faculty have been developed through the recommendations of a faculty evaluation task force. In addition, each professor or instructor has a multiyear plan of development which is reviewed every three years.

A multitude of college-initiated development opportunities has created a culture of continuous learning, motivating faculty to foster the partnering, linking, networking, and sharing necessary to the process for transformation. As one example, an annual showcase allows faculty to present their ideas and recognize innovations. A panel of peers selects the outstanding innovations, and these individuals are given an opportunity to present at the International Conference on Teaching and Leadership Conference, hosted by the National Institute for Staff and Organizational Development (NISOD).

The Central Michigan University graduate studies program has enrolled more than 200 individuals pursuing a master's degree in education. Nearly 30 "Humberites" have either completed or are pursuing a doctorate through doctoral programs in conjunction with Michigan State University and the University of Toronto (Ontario Institute for Studies in Education). Many of these have moved on to take senior posts and higher levels of responsibility at Humber and elsewhere in the college system both in Ontario and across Canada.

A model for measuring the effectiveness of instructional alternatives, such as those that emphasize a learner-centered approach or integrate the use of technology, has been developed by a faculty team. Components of the model for (course-based) instructional effectiveness include a profile of the students involved, implementation and learning process data, cost per successful completion, completion rates, entry to exit gains in the standards for the course, and comparative data for the same course run in other methods. When fully implemented, the strategy is intended to encourage experimentation; to broadly communicate the benefits, barriers, and issues associated with each approach to ensure that new experiments build on prior findings; and, hence, to systematically improve the quality of college learning services.

Program development. Curriculum is at the heart of the service provided by the college, and a learning-outcomes–based process has emerged as a result of the growing capabilities of the faculty to design and develop curriculum and instruction. External connections such as Sectoral Steering Committees—made up of employers, labour, and government representatives—are attached to schools to provide strategic advice. Program Advisory Committees provide specific curriculum advice, and more than 60 committees working with the 130 programs link the college to the world of work. The key indicator of effectiveness here is the match between the curriculum actually being implemented and the competencies needed in the job market and the workplace. The main vehicle for measuring this indicator is through the various Program Advisory Committees using college-developed program standards and/or standards set by professional associations (for example, in the fields of accounting and nursing) in conjunction with the formal program review process described below.

In the last 10 years, there has been a turnover of 40 programs and options. The rate of turnover is increasing. Informal reviews are conducted annually within each of the college academic units. A corporate resource unit with expertise in research, curriculum design, and development meets with the various units for open discussions. This review process includes inputs from advisory groups, faculty, industry, and bibliographic sources. The output of the process is an identification of new markets and ideas for modifying or developing new programs. The ideas are presented to a College Development Review Panel (CDRP) by the head of the concerned academic unit. The panel conducts a review and analysis by checking the efficacy of the proposed change or new program against the college mission and priorities (as per the annual Planning Framework, a statement of strategic direction developed with input from various working groups polling college stakeholders), funding requirements and possible financial return, and the value-added implications for the college, including the uniqueness of the program in relation to identified market niches. A decision to proceed triggers a program development cycle consisting of activities selected from an overall college model: (1) conducting a feasibility study framed by three main questions: a) "Are there work opportunities?" b) "Who would enroll in the program?" and c) "How much will it cost?"; (2) conducting job and task analyses; (3) organizing into courses and modules; and (4) preparing course outlines, learning guides, alternative approaches to instruction, and assessments.

Government-funded two- and three-year diplomas, one-year post-diploma program proposals, and all other certificate programs and courses are internally approved by the CDRP and/or the Board of Governors. Those receiving government funding are also reviewed and approved by the Ministry of Education and Training (MET), usually without major changes. The approval process at the ministry level, in reality, is mostly a "safety check" on the possible proliferation of programs among the colleges, as approval is not accompanied by capital or start-up funds.

The review process is a critical activity; thus, a Program Review task force was among the first undertakings of the newly formed Academic Council of 1982. Program review has evolved over the years and is a key mechanism for indicating the effectiveness of the college's primary service. Figure 2 illustrates the yearlong process by which programs are to be reviewed every three to five years.

A Program Review Coordinator (PRC), as indicated in Figure 2, is seconded—temporarily assigned—on a rotational basis from faculty. Decisions are made each year, using the input of the deans and the chairs regarding which programs are due for review. Data collected through the registrar regarding numbers of applications and placement of graduates help to guide the decision.

Twelve to 14 programs per year are reviewed. For each designated program, a program review committee is formed by the PRC with advice from the vice president academic, and each member is given a handbook and an orientation. In some cases, an external professional is added to the committee. Data are collected from a wide variety of sources, using various methods (see Figure 2). Survey questions have been refined over the years, and responses are computer-read to obtain fast, standardized reports. The key stakeholders in the program, including the Program Advisory Committee and any relevant professional association or standard-setting body, provide data.

The process goes through four phases, covering a period of one academic year. The crucial period between Phases II and III involves acting upon the recommendations and making changes to improve the program and close the gap between what is offered as learning outcomes via instruction and what is actually needed in the world of work.

Information generated through the process also is used for purposes of program rationalization. Budget pressures have increased the need to consider downsizing or dropping programs. In addition to effectiveness, market demand and resource use are measured. Weak programs are given four to six months to correct weaknesses, with key stakeholders involved in the discussions. During this time, the program is usually modified, and in serious cases may be restructured, downsized, or even suspended. Increasing pressures from the financial crunch and from technological and economic changes require a shorter cycle-time for review; hence, a yearly review process is being developed that will be discussed further in the final section of this chapter.

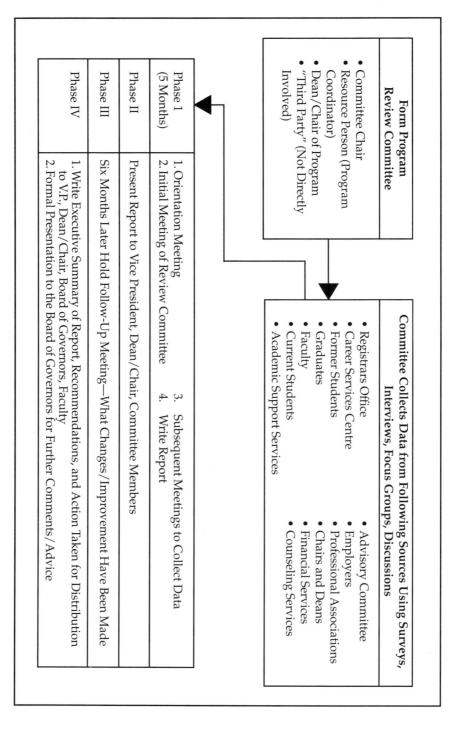

Figure 2: The Humber College Program Review Process

Resource and services development. As the college's experience and expertise with program evaluation grew, attention turned to internal, non-academic departments and units; an Operational Review process was developed for the units. Downsizing has recently placed additional pressures on many departments, making the questions of adequacy of service, cost effectiveness, and redundancy relevant collegewide.

Since 1987, over 25 operational reviews have been conducted for units such as human resources, counselling, the learning resource centres, computing services, program review, advisory committees, and the Academic Council. User satisfaction is the focus, and the structure and process are similar to that of program review.

The strengths and weaknesses of each unit are identified, and the committee makes recommendations for improvement. The recommendations are acted upon by the unit managers; after a follow-up meeting, a summary of the report and explanations of subsequent action taken are presented to the Board of Governors, the Academic Council, and the Ministry of Education and Training.

Humber was involved in a nonacademic services benchmarking project during 1994 and 1995. The key questions asked in the registration, financial, human resources, information technology, and food service areas were: how well are we doing compared to others, who is doing best and how do they do it, and how can we adapt what the best are doing and be better than the best? The benchmarking activity dealt more extensively with financial parameters and quantitative inputs and outputs of departments than does the qualitatively focussed operational review. Over 150 institutions were involved; however, very few were two-year colleges, and only three Ontario colleges participated, including Humber. The data collection instruments were designed for American institutions; hence, some of what was collected was not directly applicable to the Canadian situation. In spite of these shortcomings, Humber staff participated enthusiastically in the process-flowcharting exercises for two years, which speaks well for the readiness of the support staff and their managers in embracing the process for transformation. With limited participation from other equivalent colleges, the actual results were not as useful as was originally hoped by the vice president of administration. Nonetheless, it became apparent that benchmarking was a viable quality and effectiveness strategy for internal departments; having analyzed their processes for non-value-added procedures and possible improvements in cycle time, many units made many changes.

A next step for these departments is to conduct customer service assessments. A steering committee has been formed, and surveys are being conducted of students and college personnel—the two main user-groups of the core nonacademic departments.

Another related effectiveness strategy is Humber's policy of accepting appropriate requests from internal and external doctoral students to conduct studies within the college. The investment of staff time in these studies as interviewees or suppliers of records and documents has been well worth the benefits received through the clarifying of indicators or measures and from independent feedback that otherwise would not have been available. The Business and Industry Services and International Projects areas have both benefitted from in-depth studies; and as previously mentioned, the whole FIT system project began as a doctoral study.

Partnering. Student success is *the* critical factor of corporate success for Humber, and the forming of links, alliances, and partnerships is essential as both a means of achieving student success and as an objective for the college in its role as a global corporate citizen. As set out in "Partnerships at Humber College: A Pathway to Institutional Success" (Gordon, 1995b), the partnerships at Humber College truly constitute a pathway to institutional success.

Humber's institutionalized transformational outlook generates partnerships as a key strategy in achieving the college's mission. In fact, partnering is an aspect of the college mission itself and is seen as both a means and an end for the college. The key factor and effectiveness indicator of partnering is measured by the opportunities of which the college has availed itself. Links with business and industry through Sectoral Steering Committees and Advisory Committees, and affiliations with the League for Innovation and NISOD, have already been mentioned. Many other affiliations with professional associations and universities not only enhance staff competencies but provide critical links for students to transfer into advanced training—in spite of the official nontransfer position of the college system in Ontario—thus, enhancing student success.

As an example, Central Michigan University (CMU) is Humber's partner for offering staff the Master of Education degree program in an accessible and affordable format. Also, Humber has established an excellent reputation with foreign clients and students, particularly Malaysians. Through the longstanding partnership with CMU, a new articulation relationship is emerging for foreign students to receive credit for their three-year (practical) diploma and to be able to complete an engineering degree in less than two years at CMU. Similar arrangements already exist with other universities (for example, Penn State), and Humber has recently opened a University Centre to provide credit and noncredit courses offered through several other Canadian (for example, Sir Wilfred Laurier and Saint Mary's) and American universities.

The College Placement Test (CPT), mentioned previously, has had a significant impact on the concern for underprepared students and the diversity of language capability of the incoming students at Humber. A partnership with The College Board, originally linked through the League for Innovation, has made this intervention possible. The use of the CPT diagnostic instrument has provided the college with standards by which to validate secondary school grades, and the feedback has contributed to admissions practices adjustments.

Energies generated through the transformational process have been channeled into partnering as a major means of achieving the mission. The college, in fact, has taken advantage of many opportunities through the multitude of affiliations and partnerships that have been and continue to be established. A model for assessing the effectiveness of individual partnerships remains to be developed.

Lessons Learned and Conclusions

Customer service. Perhaps the most significant change resulting from Humber's approach to effectiveness has been the customer service orientation toward students. Persistence over time (several years in this case), using an iterative approach, was essential, as was the development of an instructional effectiveness model allowing for rational, empirical comparisons of instructional methods.

In the past, Humber was not much different from many other large public institutions—to overstate the case in making the point: "Your role and task as a student (or member of the public as the case may be) is to meet the requirements we set for you, according to our standards, or risk failure." This *in loco parentis* or "blame the victim" attitude has changed dramatically, and no group has been more surprised or more enthusiastic about the change than the students themselves, as evidenced in student satisfaction surveys and focus groups recently conducted as an element of the FIT system. Through the process for transformation and the quality/customer service approach that has been slowly introduced, the staff—and faculty, in particular—have come to see the institution and its services as having to meet the needs of students and other stakeholders (internal and external customers). The paradigm shift to the learning-centered approach, and the identification and performance assessment of learning outcomes typify this change in attitude. The shift to the learning paradigm also changes the focus of effectiveness from inputs to outputs and outcomes.

Learner attrition. The Freshman Integration and Tracking system has been nearly eight years in the making. The benefits of being able to identify real or potential problems and to intervene before the student decides to leave are fairly obvious in terms of efficiency, return on investment, and the long-term life chances of the student. Yet since the project has reached the full implementation stage, we have realized that we do not have a mechanism to interview or follow up with those who exit. Many students simply transfer from one program to another or to other institutions. Again, we do not have documentation or follow-up data. These are obvious weaknesses and must be addressed.

The feedback from computerized communications tests and FIT profiles for individual students is used to develop learning prescriptions as needed.

The resources needed to deliver remediation are significant. The college has no formal mechanism to determine the effectiveness of these remedial prescriptions. As with instructional effectiveness, a model for remedial effectiveness would provide points of comparison for making improvements and resource allocation decisions—and answer the question: "How effective is remediation?" The question can be expanded to the whole area of student progress after the first year: "How effective are the interventions we provide such as peer tutoring, study skills workshops, counselling, assigning students to learning teams, and other experiences, including the library and the open learning centres?" If the student passes the course or the program, we assume such interventions and learning services were and are effective; but to date we have not developed measures to determine if that is an accurate assumption.

Professional competence. The transformational process of growing and developing a skill base among staff simultaneously requires an attitudinal shift and the provision of learning opportunities. Fostering the awareness among staff that further skill acquisition is needed and the knowledge that they are both capable of doing so and have access to skill enhancement are essential complementary phenomena for raising consciousness, shifting perceptions, and "kick-starting" the process. By encouraging staff to work in teams, while also providing secondment and international consulting and teaching opportunities, the college has helped make effectiveness pursuits possible through transformation. A comprehensive program of holding conferences, providing job exchange and secondment opportunities, offering an M.Ed. and Ph.D. program, and all of the activities of NISOD and the League for Innovation have helped to foster an awareness of development needs, the realization of capability, and the assurance of opportunity. A recent initiative that provides mentoring for part-time continuing education instructors is a prime example of how the intellectual and experiential capital of transformation can be effectively accumulated.

Although faculty surveys have been conducted over the years, the college has been somewhat remiss in systematically and regularly collecting data on staff satisfaction. Given the facts that the faculty are unionized and that there have been two systemwide strikes, albeit in a 30-year period, data and information on satisfaction levels would be significant aids in judging and improving effectiveness of the human resource and professional development activities and transformational processes of the college.

Program development and funding. Programming and provincial college funding are inextricably interdependent. The traditional teaching-centered approach to curriculum design, development, delivery, and assessment is reflected by the funding formula for determining the provincial funding (60 percent of total operating revenue) to colleges. On a particular day of the semester, the numbers of registered students in each program are worked into a formula for that program. Currently, each college's funding is based on

a three-year average of enrollment divided by the three-year average enrollment of the entire system. This year's numbers of students influence what
will be received as a grant three years hence. Because each college's share of
the declining levels of provincial funding is based on "market share," the
model encourages both growth and efficiency.

As the college moves to a learning-centered approach based on learning
outcomes, the funding process will have to move to an output model or performance-based funding. Accountability is now shifting from providing
instruction to producing learning. Funding also should be based on measures
of what actually was produced—in other words, funding for learning outcomes achieved. The prerequisites to this fiscal arrangement are clear sets of
learning outcomes and valid, reliable means of evaluating student achievement or performance for each program. The measures are related to the success of students and their ability to demonstrate outcomes and build relevant
careers. A caveat with respect to performance-based funding is the potential
for raising the entry qualifications to increase the probability of success in
meeting exit standards (for example, there may be no grant given for students
who do not demonstrate full competence). The trend would be toward elit-
ism while the capability of the college to work with diverse entry skills would
be dissipated. Any new funding policy would have to take this possibility
into consideration.

Institutionalizing the program review process. Humber's administration
has learned that there is a long-term cumulative effect of systematic program
review. Faculty and program administrators have come to accept regular
review as an essential way of doing business. Each program or school is now
being asked to conduct an independent annual review, as the next development and use of the organizational capital accumulated through the process
of program evaluations. The level of accountability in the program area can
be raised by shortening the review cycle time from five years to one year and
engaging experienced faculty who are committed to the evaluation process.

The many years of experience of conducting program review have yielded a set of criteria which, as indicators, are measurable, available, relevant
against benchmarks, reliable, and clear. These are: 1) program effectiveness in
terms of attrition rate, employer and student satisfaction, curriculum relevance, learning outcomes demonstrated by exiting students, and the currency and adequacy of resources needed for the program; 2) demand for graduates as measured by job placements, graduate retention in employment, and
graduate advancement; 3) student demand as measured by applications over
a three-year period; and 4) cost effectiveness and resource use. These are
intended for collegewide application in the 1996-97 academic year.

Instructional effectiveness and modularization. With the increasing use
and integration of technology and the thrust toward a learning-centered paradigm, the need for modularized learning experiences and units is also accel-

erating. By packaging learning experiences around learning outcomes, the
college can implement alternative modes of learning such as the use of learn-
ing-resource centres; open learning centres; home study; self-directed learning teams; mixing and matching of learning outcomes to meet the specific
needs of learners; self-pacing; and the integration of educational technology
such as CD-ROM, computer conferencing, tutorial by electronic mail, and
video conferencing. All of these modes of learning can be supported by a
growing set of software tools for managing the instructional process, developing and administering tests, developing instructional packages, and providing information.

The success of students in demonstrating learning outcomes is the measure of the effectiveness of program development. All programs have stated
methods whereby the outcomes of each course can be measured, but there
has been no formal evaluation of the effectiveness of these processes, something which must be carried out soon.

Developing new partnerships. Given that partnering has been and is one
of Humber's "pathways to institutional success," striking up partnerships
without strategic intent is not effective. All markets can be segmented in various ways. Since the college cannot be all things to all people, the lesson is to
search out market niches and aggressively pursue them to establish domi-
nance through customer service and willingness to target our intellectual,
professional, and cultural capital. For example, seeing ourselves as a suppli-
er of quality curriculum and technologically integrated learning experiences,
one market niche to be explored and nurtured is that of publishing companies. A measure of the indicator of the effectiveness of forming partnerships
as stated in the mission is the recent alliance developed with McGraw Hill
publishers to joint-venture educational "learningware" used to supplement
learning modules.

To accelerate the ability of the college to push aggressively into these new
niches, a Staff Computer Training Facility was established as an open
resource and support for all staff to acquire and upgrade their computer
skills. Also, Humber has targeted $200,000 annually to provide computers to
faculty teams with priority needs. Coupled with a program to provide inter-
est-free, payroll-deductible loans for the purchase of computer work stations
and software, Humber staff are visibly supported in their efforts to achieve
computer competencies. These competencies, in turn, have been used to
develop superior curriculum and learning materials which have caught the
eye of a major educational publisher. Other publishers have shown interest,
and the alliances are growing. Given Humber's limited experience with dis-
tance education programming, these alliances can be catalysts for the college
to become more effective in the distance-delivery modes.

To a large extent, "effectiveness is in the eye of the beholder." Each stakeholder group looks from its own perspective. Government and the public-at-

large focus on financial accountability and inputs: Are public funds being used in the most efficient way to provide education and job preparation? At the same time, the students, college faculty, and administration are looking at outputs and outcomes: Do graduates have the competencies at the standards expected by employers and professional associations? Are these graduates satisfied and launched in careers creating and maintaining the national economy? Concomitantly, effectiveness and its measures cascade through the organization and must be understood contextually through analysis, interpretation, and the needs of the audience for the resulting information. Given the current state of our information-handling capability, the collecting, processing, reporting, and interpreting of effectiveness measurement data are rapidly becoming "taken-for-granteds." Promptly acting on that information has become a way of doing business in the college.

Humber's organic approach to effectiveness for over a decade has focussed on human resource and organizational development in an evolving milieu of customer service, participation, innovation, and partnering. The process for transformation has developed and prepared the corporate culture and social infrastructure to the point where the college can cope with serious crises and at the same time take full advantage of information technology tools for processing data and information—and for establishing reference points for comparison purposes. The integration of cooperative workgroups and more friendly technological applications of software and hardware into "groupware" is providing an emerging framework for measuring effectiveness that responds to the differing roles, levels, needs, and perceptions of the various stakeholder groups.

Humber's acknowledged position as a leader in providing quality learning experiences has been earned by adopting strategies aimed at fostering a concern for people, processes, flexibility, and empowering practices. But, healthy evolution can be guaranteed only if complacency regarding past success is not allowed to become institutionalized. Continuous review and assessment through forums and cross-functional teams, task forces, and steering committees must be constantly utilized to create, energize, and implement new challenges and opportunities. Most important is the process itself. While drawing upon the perpetually renewing human capital generated by the process for transformation, the process can support and guide the college in developing quality activities that can continuously be measured and enhanced in the never-ending search for institutional effectiveness.

The author acknowledges with thanks the contributions made by Humber College staff, Roy Giroux and Richard Hook, and particularly, William Sinnett.

BACKGROUND

A large, public, urban, comprehensive, multicampus college of applied arts and technology located in Toronto (Canada's most populous city, with approximately three million people), Humber College of Applied Arts and Technology is one in a system of 25 colleges within the Province of Ontario. Since its inception in 1967, Humber has grown to be one of the largest colleges in Canada with over 11,000 full-time students, 70,000 part-time, 1,000 full-time personnel, and an operating budget of over $100 million.

The 130 programs and more than 1,000 courses encompass short-term certificates, two- and three-year diplomas, and one-year post-diploma learning opportunities. Continuing education and contract training departments provide extensive learning services to the part-time students.

Each of the 10 provinces and two territories in Canada has jurisdiction over its own educational system; hence, with no central governmental authority in the field of education, there are 12 separate systems. Within the Ontario provincial educational system, the colleges are distinct from and parallel to the universities. There is no standardized policy on the transfer from college to university, but institution-specific articulation efforts and agreements are receiving increased attention.

Each Ontario college provides services within a specific geographical area. Humber, being one of four Toronto colleges, is located at the western "growing edge" of the city; having a comparatively limited geographical area of responsibility, it draws nearly 80 percent of its students from beyond its boundaries—making a residence an essential facility.

The college is responsible to the Ministry of Education and Training through a semi-autonomous Board of Governors with external members being appointed and four internal representatives being elected. The president is a voting member of the board. There have been only two presidents in Humber's 30-year history—the incumbent has been in office since 1982.

Full-time faculty and support staff each belong to their own unions. Restructuring in 1994 reduced the number of academic deans, reorganizing the traditional academic discipline divisions (technology, business, health, applied arts) into 12 schools along economic sector lines (for example, manufacturing and design, social and community services, hospitality, business, and media), with individual schools being headed by an academic chair.

REFERENCES

Academic Vice Presidents. "Learning-Centered Education in Ontario's Colleges." A white paper prepared for the Council of Presidents. Toronto: Association of Colleges of Applied Arts and Technology of Ontario, 1995.

Barr, R.B. and Tagg, J. "From Teaching to Learning: A New Paradigm for Undergraduate Education." *Change*, November/December 1995, 13-25.

College Standards and Accreditation Council. "The Accreditation of College Programs: A Discussion Paper." Toronto: College Standards and Accreditation Council, 1996.

Gordon, R.A. "Can Community Colleges Do the Job?" *Leadership Abstracts*, August 1995a, *8* (8), 1-2.

Gordon, R.A. "Partnerships at Humber College: A Pathway to Institutional Success." In J.E. Roueche, L.S. Taber, and S.D. Roueche (Eds.), *The Company We Keep: Collaboration in the Community College*. Washington, DC: The Community College Press, 1995b, 107-127.

Information Technology Task Force. "Final Report of the Humber College Task Force on Information Technology." Toronto: Humber College of Applied Arts and Technology, 1995.

Office of Research and Planning, Association of Colleges of Applied Arts and Technology of Ontario. "Accountability in a Learning-Centered Environment: Using Performance Indicators in Reporting, Advocacy and Planning." A discussion paper prepared for the colleges of applied arts and technology of Ontario. Toronto: ACAATO, 1996.

Chapter IX

The final contributed chapter, by George Boggs, superintendent/president of Palomar College (CA), brings us full circle. The first contribution (Chapter 3), by Hudgins and Williams, described the reality and the power of a viable, developing, strengthening paradigm shift. They began with the shift in public thinking about college practice and effectiveness, and described broadly the implications and current results of that shift. Boggs describes yet another developing paradigm shift—from the traditional teaching to the more contemporary learning paradigm.

Using that shift as the backdrop for his discussion, Boggs describes the steps in Palomar's progress toward a recasting of its vision and rewording of its mission statement, including—as did McClenney and Gordon, in particular—the important contribution of the environmental scan. As did Hudgins and Williams, Boggs notes that standards by which community colleges have been judged in the past (typical of four-year colleges and universities) never were nor ever will be appropriate standards for future evaluations. He recommends establishing focused committees with distinct planning and operational responsibilities, writing clear goals and focused outcome measures, and supporting the learning paradigm shift by keeping improved student learning at the heart of the effectiveness model. Further, he warns that resistance to leadership efforts to reinforce the need to be accountable for meeting the goals and objectives of newly cast college mission statements is not uncommon, even among those who have committed in principle and by vote to the support and evaluation of effectiveness practices.

George R. Boggs
Superintendent/President
Palomar College
San Marcos, California

A Shared Vision for Learning Outcome Improvements at Palomar College

Shared visions derive their power from a common caring…one of the reasons people seek to build shared visions is their desire to be connected in an important undertaking.
—P.M. Senge, 1990, *The Fifth Discipline*

The community colleges in California were swept into a protracted period of change beginning in 1978 with the passage of the California Property Tax Limitation Initiative (Proposition 13). Perhaps the most significant effect of this ballot initiative was the transfer of authority and funding away from local districts to the state. Locally elected boards of trustees, accountable to the electorate of local districts, no longer had the authority to establish property tax assessments for the colleges nor to establish fees for students. As responsibility for financing community colleges was shifted to the state, the California legislature and the governor reacted to limit state expenditures through such actions as de-funding of courses which were considered by the state to be frivolous, the enactment of uniform student enrollment fees, and state-imposed enrollment caps on local districts. The State Board of Governors was charged with monitoring the local districts for compliance with new state regulations.

Community college legislative reform. In the early 1980s, the California legislature became concerned about the governance of the community colleges and about the fiscal accountability of the local community college districts. As a consequence of state-imposed enrollment fees, enrollment caps, and de-funding of certain courses, enrollment dropped significantly at community colleges throughout the state; and, by 1983, the financial stability of many of the districts was in question. Some were on the verge of bankruptcy and had petitioned the state for assistance. Others were forced to lay off faculty and staff. In some districts, faculty and staff became active in the election of local board members who promised to protect employee rights. Since collective bargaining and employee salary and benefit expenditures were still controlled by local governing boards, some legislators questioned the fiscal responsibility of certain local districts.

By 1984, the Commission for Review of the Master Plan for Higher Education in California had completed a Community College Reassessment Study and forwarded it to the Legislative Joint Committee for the Review of the Master Plan. In 1986, the governor signed Assembly Bill 3409, which required the chancellor of the California Community Colleges to develop a new state-supported allocation system for community colleges and to conduct a study on developing and implementing a statewide program of educational accountability. The law went so far as to specify the composition of some advisory task forces, reflecting the increasing statewide influence of faculty through the Academic Senate of the California Community Colleges.

Assembly Bill 1725, passed in 1988 after several years of review by the legislature, established the California Community Colleges as the state's third system of public higher education. The University of California and the California State University had already been designated as state systems by the California Master Plan for Higher Education. As a consequence of this new designation as a state system, the legislature, in the Community College Reform Act of 1988, began to ask for greater accountability to the state. In fact, one of the provisions of AB 1725 stated, "The board of governors shall develop and implement a comprehensive community college educational and fiscal accountability system."

Accountability laws. Laws passed by the California Legislature between 1986 and 1988 asked the Community College System to develop a reporting mechanism which would define and measure, quantitatively and qualitatively, specified accountability information. Requested information included student access to community colleges; the extent to which the statewide community college student body proportionately reflected the adult population of the state; student transfer rates, academic standards, and student achievement; student goal satisfaction and success in courses and programs; completion rates of courses and programs; occupational preparation relative to state and local workforce needs and for entry-level employment, occupational advancement, and career changes; adequacy of basic skills and English-as-a-second-language instruction in preparing students to succeed in college-level work; adequacy of, and student satisfaction with, student services; the extent to which the community college workforce proportionately reflects the adult population of the state; and the fiscal condition of the local districts.

California was not alone in its interest in accountability for higher education. A 1989 survey conducted for the National Governor's Association found that 36 states had implemented or were considering implementing some form of accountability system. Ironically, what the states mandated were not outcomes so much as processes (Ewell, 1992). That proved to be true in California as well; the education code mandates processes and procedures which have not been shown to affect student learning outcomes.

The 1988 legislation in California required the California Community College Board of Governors to implement a comprehensive accountability system over a three-year period beginning no later than the 1991-92 academic year. In order to develop such a system, the Chancellor of the California Community Colleges convened the AB 1725 Accountability Task Force on November 10, 1989.

The Accountability Task Force. At the July 1990 meeting of the Board of Governors of the California Community Colleges, the Accountability Task Force introduced its Model Accountability System. The model described the use of indicators to document the system's institutional effectiveness in meeting its postsecondary obligations. The task force members were concerned that the model system should recognize the differences between the individual colleges and that any reporting mechanisms be coordinated with existing reporting requirements. The task force wanted to make certain that indicators of institutional effectiveness related to the mission statements of the system and the individual colleges.

The model developed by the task force contained five major components: student access, student success, student satisfaction, staff composition, and fiscal condition. A number of specific data elements were detailed in the report of the task force. Full implementation of the Model Accountability System was contingent upon securing adequate funding in the 1991-92 California Budget Act, since the new state community college system did not have a management information system adequate to handle the collection, analysis, and reporting of the suggested data elements. Due to the economic recession which dramatically reduced state revenues, an adequate management information system has not yet been funded, and the legislatively mandated accountability system, for the most part, has been on hold.

Accreditation changes. Regional accreditation has always been in the business of institutional assessment. In the past, however, accreditation self-studies and reports of team visits focused upon institutional resources and processes. A growing interest on the part of the public and legislative bodies influenced accrediting agencies to assign a greater emphasis to measures of institutional effectiveness. The Accrediting Commission for Community and Junior Colleges of the Western Association of Colleges and Schools was no exception. Each iteration of the standard on assessment of the outcomes of instruction was increasingly assertive (Petersen, 1990). Revisions of the accreditation standards in 1990, and again in 1996, required greater attention to an institution's development of means for evaluating how well and in what ways it is accomplishing its purposes. Evaluation teams were also instructed to look for evidence that the results of these evaluations were used as the basis for broad-based, continuous planning and improvement. In its guide for self-study, the commission states that outcome measures used in program review should be described and evaluated in terms of the mission of the institution and the students it serves. The focus should be on learning, not simply on providing programs and services. A specific standard addresses effectiveness and planning.

Association efforts. From 1987 through 1989, the president of Palomar College served as chair of the Commission on Research for the California Association of Community Colleges (CACC). A major focus of the commission in those years was institutional effectiveness. In 1988, CACC published a report of the Research Commission, *Indicators and Measures of Successful Community Colleges*; and in 1989, CACC published *Criteria and Measures of Institutional Effectiveness*. Although these reports did not focus solely on learning outcome measures as the most important indicators, it was clear that community college leaders in California were determined to develop methods to document the effectiveness of the colleges. A spring 1989 article in *Trustee Quarterly* discussed the role of trustees in assessing institutional effectiveness and referred to the interest in college effectiveness on the parts of the American Association of Community and Junior Colleges, the Association of Community College Trustees, and the nation's accreditation commissions (Giles and Slark, 1989).

The Process

At Palomar College, 1989 was a time for rediscovery. At the national level, the American Association of Community and Junior Colleges had just issued the report of its Commission on the Future of Community Colleges, *Building Communities: A Vision for a New Century* (AACJC, 1988), calling on colleges to expand access, to improve retention of students, to form new partnerships and alliances, to develop a core of common learning, and to build a climate of community. At the state level, the California Legislature had just passed AB 1725, the comprehensive Community College Reform Act. Funding for the colleges was now centralized and program-based, and the colleges were being asked to be accountable for the expenditure of scarce resources. The fiscal health of local districts was being monitored closely by the State Chancellor's Office.

At the local level, Palomar College found itself in a dynamic environment. The communities it served were among the fastest-growing in the country. College leaders and the Governing Board were challenged to find ways to make classes accessible to the people of the college's large and rapidly growing district without overburdening the San Marcos campus. In addition, the California State University system had chosen to build its twentieth campus just two miles from the San Marcos campus of Palomar College, raising concern about the impact that the university would have on Palomar's mission.

The nature of the college's student body was also changing—becoming, on the average, older, more female, and more economically and socially diverse. Assessment tests revealed increased weaknesses in basic skills abilities. English-as-a-second-language classes and developmental courses in mathematics, reading, and English became the college's fastest-growing offerings. Everything around the college—from the local, state, and national environments to its students—seemed to be changing. Would the college be prepared for the future, and how could it influence what that future might be?

The Vision Task Force. It was in this environment that the college president convened and chaired the Vision Task Force. The charge for the group was to develop a proposed vision statement for the college, to look into the future, and to envision what the college should be in 2005. This 16-member task force was comprised of representatives from all segments of the college and one community member. The vice president of the Associated Student Government and a member of the Governing Board joined faculty members, administrators, and other staff members in an adventure which would last 18 months.

The founders of the college, which had opened its doors in 1946 to 198 students, probably would not have imagined that it would grow by 1989 to enroll 22,000 students in nearly 130 different degree and certificate programs at the San Marcos campus, at seven education centers, and at more than 60 other locations scattered throughout a district larger than Rhode Island or Delaware. Too often, institutions are so busy keeping up with the demands of the present that they are not able to see a future that is any different. The charge of the Vision Task Force, however, was to imagine what the college would look like 16 years in the future.

Project activities. The Vision Task Force began its work by studying documents about the challenges and roles of community colleges and about the economic and social trends in the country, state, and communities served by the college. The members read *Building Communities*, reports which led to the California Community College Reform Act, articles on strategic planning, and articles on classroom assessment. They reviewed vision statements from businesses and from other colleges and universities. They surveyed and interviewed faculty, staff, students, and selected community members. They asked business owners in the communities served by the college how many new employees they would need in the next 16 years and what skills future employees would need. They interviewed presidents of local colleges and universities to see what plans neighboring institutions of higher education had for their futures.

Environmental scan. Data were also gathered from local, county, state, and national governments, public schools, and local planning agencies. The task force was interested in population projections and the special needs of that population. The members wanted to know whether potential students would need English language or citizenship skills, whether there would be more single-parent households, and what the age and ethnic mix of the population would be. The task force members were also concerned about changes in transportation arteries. Based upon its findings, the task force developed a set of assumptions about the environment in the future.

Next, the task force critically assessed the college's strengths and weaknesses. The members wanted to know both what the college did well and what could be done better. The task force members discussed at length their own values and their own aspirations for the future of the college, how the college did its work, and the nature of its contributions to the community and society. After 18 months of study, discussion, and work, the task force issued its proposed vision statement and a revised mission statement to the college community. Having concluded its work, the task force was disbanded.

The vision statement. In the foreword to the vision statement document issued in 1991, the college president wrote:

> Readers of these statements will note that they reflect a subtle but nonetheless profound shift in how we think of the college and what we do. We have shifted from an identification with process to an identification with results. We are no longer content with merely providing quality instruction. We will judge ourselves henceforth on the quality of student learning we produce. And further, we will judge ourselves by our ability to produce even greater and more sophisticated student learning and meaningful educational success with each passing year, each exiting student, and each graduating class. To do this, we must ourselves continually experiment, discover, grow, and learn. Consequently, we see ourselves as a learning institution in both our object and our method. (Boggs, 1991, p. 1)

The new mission and vision statements clearly established Palomar College as a learning college. The five themes of the statements—empowerment, learning, evaluation, discovery, and growth—all focused on student learning. Under the empowerment theme, the vision statement proclaimed, "Palomar College empowers students to learn and empowers our educational team—faculty, staff, and administration—to create powerful learning environments." Under the learning theme, the vision statement reads, in part, "We provide an environment where persons of diverse cultural and ethnic backgrounds become partners in learning, build on the strengths of their own cultural traditions, and respect, embrace, and learn from persons of other traditions." Under the evaluation theme, Palomar College says it "judges its work and its programs and formulates its policies primarily on the basis of learning outcomes." Under the discovery theme, the vision statement commits Palomar College to discovering "new and better ways to enhance learning." Under the growth theme, the college says it will continue "to build on its strengths and shape its growth to promote more efficient and effective learning."

When the proposed vision statement was presented to the college constituencies, it was approved without much discussion or even realization of its significance by the Faculty Senate, the Administrative Association, the Associated Student Government, and the Council of Classified Employees. On February 12, 1991, the Governing Board adopted the vision statement and the new mission statement as official college policy.

A paradigm shift. Members of the Vision Task Force were surprised to find such easy acceptance of a dramatic change in the college mission and direction. The task force had asked the institution to take responsibility for student learning, not just for delivering instruction, and there was no opposition! Some speculated that people thought that the vision statement would find a comfortable resting place on a shelf and business would continue as usual. Or perhaps people felt that this emphasis on learning outcomes was just another passing fad to be endured. What the task force members think is the real answer came to them as they viewed Joel Arthur Barker's videotape on paradigms. Task force members came to believe that people are blinded to the need to change because they are operating from a different paradigm of community colleges, one which college leaders have labeled the "instruction paradigm." In 1991, the new paradigm envisioned by the Palomar College vision statement began to be called the "learning paradigm" by college leaders.

A paradigm, as most natural scientists and now a growing number of business leaders know, is a pattern or a model—in particular, an outstandingly clear or typical example or archetype. A paradigm is a way of understanding and making sense of information about a subject. When people are functioning within a system, one can say that they are operating according to its paradigm. As futurist Barker reminds us, a paradigm includes rules and regulations that establish boundaries, provide rules for success within the boundaries, and act as filters for data. What is obvious to people within a paradigm may be invisible to people outside of it, and vice versa.

Palomar College leaders knew it would not be easy to change the paradigm that guided the college from one of providing instruction to one of producing student learning. But they began a series of activities to start on the path to change, beginning with the language used. As a result of the work of the Vision Task Force, the college had a new mission statement which defined its purpose as student learning. Next, catalogs, publications, and job descriptions were changed. For example, the job description of the instructional deans was revised to include responsibility for creating effective learning environments for students. Student service deans now are expected to develop and evaluate the performance of assigned personnel in terms of their contributions to student learning and success.

Recruitment brochures were revised to attract a faculty and staff committed to promoting and supporting student learning. Employment procedures were revised to help select faculty and staff who shared the college's values and beliefs. Orientation programs for new full- and part-time faculty and new members of the Governing Board now emphasize the principles of the learning paradigm.

Student learning forums which brought together faculty, staff, and students were scheduled. These forums are based upon the conviction that if faculty and staff listen carefully to students and respond appropriately to their suggestions, student learning and student success can be improved. For example, in 1993-94, there were three such forums at Palomar College. The first was facilitated by students who focused on positive and negative classroom and campus experiences, and on successful techniques that helped them learn.

The second student learning forum was facilitated by faculty and the college president. Its goal was to review the negative experiences identified in the first forum and to develop suggestions to counteract them. The ESL faculty facilitated the third forum, "How to Engage Your Students From Day One." The third forum focused on techniques for assessing student understanding from the first day of class and on improving communications with students.

Since 1993, Palomar College staff members have written numerous professional articles and made more than 30 presentations about the learning paradigm at individual colleges and at conferences, including six keynote presentations. Palomar College staff participated in two national video conferences on the learning paradigm in 1995.

Feedback from these presentations and articles has helped college leaders to clarify their thinking. It has also reinforced the belief in the need to shift to the learning paradigm. An added benefit has been the effect on the reputation of the college. Faculty and staff members who attend conferences are frequently asked by colleagues from other colleges about the innovations at Palomar. When they return, they are not only proud of what is being accomplished at Palomar, but they are even more committed to the paradigm shift. Moreover, an article in the *AACC Community College Journal* listed Palomar College as one of three flagship community colleges for its emphasis on student learning (O'Banion, 1995-96).

As a result of a newspaper editorial on the effective use of technology to improve learning outcomes (Tagg, 1995), *Encyclopedia Britannica* asked Palomar College to be the first community college to pilot-test its Britannica-on-Line service. Faculty members experimented with the Britannica-on-Line database during the fall semester of 1995; and, in the spring of 1996, the database was used by students in selected classes through the Internet.

The Institutional Effectiveness Model

The learning paradigm clearly focuses Palomar College on student learning, measurement of student learning outcomes, and setting goals for improvement of those outcomes. However, leaders of the college readily admit that the college has a long way to go to realize its vision. A frank discussion of the progress of the college is reported in the *Institutional Self-Study for Reaffirmation of Accreditation* (Barkley, Mozes, Raos and Associates, 1996) and in the superintendent/president's *1995/96 Year in Review* (Boggs, 1996).

Internal governance. The current governance structure at Palomar College was adopted in 1989, after nearly two years of study. In accordance with the college values, the governance structure provides for a comprehensive planning process that involves all segments of the college community. In creating the governance structure, college leaders consciously separated strategic planning committees from operational committees in order to prevent short-term operational issues from driving planning committee agendas.

Institutional planning. The planning process uses the results of institutional research. The director of institutional research and planning is an ex-officio member of the Educational Master Planning Committee (EMPC) and works closely with the vice president for instruction to provide information, research, and analytical support to all planning committees. The college's *FactBook* (Barr, 1995), containing a wide variety of 10-year historical statistical information, research summaries, and analytical studies, is available to and used by the planning committees.

Palomar College has five strategic planning committees and a number of standing and ad hoc operational planning committees. The committees for instructional planning, student services planning, facilities planning, and staff planning report to the EMPC. The EMPC, chaired by the assistant superintendent/vice president for instruction, reports to the superintendent/president who involves the board in planning activities each year at a goal-setting retreat. The other planning committees are chaired by the appropriate vice president, except the Instructional Planning Committee which is chaired by an instructional dean and a faculty member. Each planning committee is composed of administrators, faculty, staff, and students appointed by their respective constituent groups.

From time to time, ad hoc, broad-based planning task forces are created by the EMPC to conduct in-depth studies and to make strategic recommendations regarding a particular issue. For example, in response to a directive from the superintendent/president, the EMPC created a Technology Planning Task Force in 1995-96 in order to develop a strategic technology plan for the college. The technology plan will be incorporated into the college's educational master plan.

The five strategic planning committees have been functioning for the past six years. They have studied many issues and made recommendations about a broad range of strategic planning issues. Their work is summarized and updated annually in the college's five-year Educational Master Plan. This 115-page document contains a brief description of the college, external environmental planning assumptions, five-year goals and plans, current recommendations, a tracking of implementation actions, and a five-year resource allocation plan.

Learning outcomes. The vision statement focuses the college on student learning and on evaluations based upon student learning outcomes. Key to the establishment of learning outcome goals is the identification of the core knowledge and skills that Palomar College graduates must demonstrate. The Governing Board Goals for 1995-96 clearly supported the development of core knowledge and skills requirements.

Following the Board's direction, the Instructional Planning Committee, on recommendations from its Core Knowledge and Skills Subcommittee, has drafted general definitions of abilities that all students who complete a course of study at Palomar College will possess. The committee incorporated the competencies included in the Secretary's Commission on Achieving Necessary Skills (SCANS) report (1991) and identified the nature of language proficiencies that students will possess. The subcommittee continues to work on defining abilities and determining ways to measure how successful individual students have been at acquiring them. These recommendations are scheduled to be forwarded to EMPC next year.

Program review. A systematic program review process in the standard sense has not existed at Palomar College for more than 11 years. Program review groups in the past were seen as focusing on program elimination and, therefore, were viewed with suspicion. Nonetheless, all of the information and studies typically generated for program review have been regularly and systematically prepared and used at the college. After several years of absence, an Institutional Review Committee was formed at Palomar College in spring 1996 to develop policies and procedures for conducting regular and comprehensive review of all programs and services, to ensure all were in compliance with the college mission and the Educational Master Plan, and to make recommendations to improve efficiency and effectiveness of all programs.

Student outcomes information has been developed for instructional programs, including studies of course completion rates; the tracking of 10 first-time college cohorts for persistence and completion; the assessment of effectiveness of learning communities, basic skills computer labs, and linked courses. A study was conducted on the effectiveness of four-unit versus three-unit Intermediate Algebra courses on student performance in the subsequent college algebra course.

Vocational programs receive additional review and evaluation. Vocational follow-up studies ask former students a series of questions about their educational experiences. Nursing education, dental assisting, and emergency medical training programs are evaluated routinely by their professional regulatory agencies, and graduates of these programs must pass externally generated qualifying examinations. Vocational Technology Advisory Committees help to keep the college on track with the needs of industry and business, frequently recommending appropriate program revisions.

Student service programs are also subject to external program review from the State Chancellor's Office. The Palomar College Matriculation Program and the Extended Opportunities Programs and Services were the subject of a Technical Assistance Site Visit in 1996. Both programs were found to be sound by state standards.

Intervention research. Research studies, conducted by Palomar College's Office of Institutional Research and Planning, reveal that students who participate in certain activities are much more likely to be successful and to persist in college than is the student body in general. For example, 75 percent of the students who complete the college matriculation process of basic skills assessment, college orientation, advisement, and counseling persist to the second semester. The comparison figure for non-matriculants is 39 percent. Students who complete a College Success Skills class in their first semester persist at a rate of 83 percent compared to a 58 percent persistence rate for all students. Overall, students who are somehow attached to a student service program (for example, financial aid, extended opportunities programs and services, veterans' services, or disabled students programs and services) are at least 52 percent more likely to persist and to complete their educational goals than those who are not (Barkley et al., 1996, p. 72). Student athletes are 48 percent more likely to persist to the second semester than are other students.

Student equity. The Palomar College Student Equity Plan (Weldele and associates, 1995) is an effort to review learning outcomes for students in designated demographic groups, to set goals to reduce disparities, and to improve outcomes for all groups. The plan identifies goals, barriers to goal accomplishment, activities designed to accomplish the goal, groups or individuals responsible for implementation of the goal, an expected date of completion, and an identified source of funding.

The five goals listed in the Palomar College Student Equity Plan commit the college to ensuring that college enrollment reflects the percentage of each group in the adult population of the communities served, to increasing the successful completion of basic skills and ESL courses, to increasing the successful completion of college courses, to increasing the successful completion of programs leading to degrees and certificates, and to increasing transfer rates to upper-division colleges and universities. Historical data are provided in the plan by student gender and ethnic category along with goals for improvement.

Feedback information. Palomar College regularly receives data from the California State University system on the success of transfer students after one semester. The college also sends information to local high schools on the success of their graduates who attend Palomar. Data from the California State University system indicate that students who transfer from Palomar College achieve higher grades after transferring than do the native university students.

The Palomar College *FactBook* (Barr, 1995) is a rich source of information on community demographics and projections; local school district enrollments and graduates; college enrollment statistics; degrees, certificates, and characteristics of associate degree graduates; transfers to the University of California and to California State University; employee statistics; employee climate; college finances; campus facilities; studies of students fully certified for transfer; average weekly student contact hours per full-time-equivalent faculty member by department; persistence and performance of entering student cohorts; college course success rates by basic skill course and by assessment test scores; and an enrollment summary by division and discipline.

Lessons Learned and Conclusions

Leading a college in refocusing on measurable outcomes and increasing effectiveness is not an easy task. Most colleges have been in existence for some time and have strong, established cultures. All too often, universities are viewed as models for what community colleges should become. In a university, the responsibility for learning is usually considered to be the student's and not the university's. The criteria for judging the quality of universities are almost always based upon inputs and process measures rather than outcomes. For example, factors such as selectivity of student admissions, number of library holdings, size of endowments, and number of doctorates on the faculty are commonly used measures at colleges and universities.

Educators traditionally have resisted efforts to measure outcomes, sometimes referring to measures of efficiency and effectiveness as more appropriate to business than to education. Others are afraid that they might be compared inappropriately to other institutions of higher education which serve different student bodies or have different missions. However, in an environment of scarce resources, the public and the elected officials want to know what they are receiving for their money. If institutions of higher education do not establish clear outcome goals and ways to measure them, these goals and measurements may be imposed by state governments. Leaders at Palomar College believe it is time for a new paradigm, one in which community colleges will be the models, and one in which colleges will be evaluated based upon measurable contributions to student learning and success.

College governance. Most colleges have an abundance of committees. With shared governance, it appears that every constituency wants to have a say in the decisions which affect their institution. Colleges, however, are not always clear about how these groups interface or how they contribute to the overall governance of the institution. Moreover, committees tend to drift toward dealing with operational issues which might be more appropriately handled administratively.

Committees are most valuable in helping to plan for the future of the college if they are assigned responsibility for planning and if agendas are developed so that operational issues do not crowd out the time needed for effective planning. At Palomar College, operational and planning committees are separated so that the planning committees are not distracted by operational issues.

The ultimate authority for local college governance is usually an elected or appointed governing board of trustees. The mission of a board of trustees, according to Nason (1982, p. 19), is to act as guardians of the college mission. They must make sure that the institution's programs conform to its stated purpose and that college funds are spent in support of the mission and the shared vision for the future of the college. When internal constituencies become too focused on current operational or short-term problems, college presidents should be able to count on trustees to insist on long-term planning.

Mission clarity. Institutional effectiveness has little meaning if a college is not clear about its purpose. College leaders need to review mission statements and to review or develop vision statements for the future of their colleges. Only if an institution knows what its outcomes should be and what it wants its future to be will it be able to ascertain whether it is effective and whether it is making progress.

Once the college has a mission statement and a vision for its future which are endorsed by the college community, it can identify the outcomes that need to be measured. Goals for improving outcome measures can be set, and timetables for achieving those goals can be established.

Colleges must also establish a means to collect and to analyze outcomes data. More and more colleges are establishing offices for institutional research and planning. Management information systems have to be in place for the systematic collection and reporting of information. Colleges without mechanisms in place for the collection and analysis of data will not be able to assess their effectiveness as an institution.

Of course, data and information are of no value if they are not related to the mission and vision of the institution or if the data and information are not used in planning or decisionmaking. In particular, college leaders need to develop a resource allocation plan that is in alignment with its mission, vision, and educational master plan. College innovators should be supported, and departments which can prove their progress in improving identified outcome measures should be rewarded.

Design principles. According to an accountability guide prepared by Far West Laboratories for the California Community College Chancellor's Office (undated, p. 4), a successful accountability system must collect data that show how the college ensures student access, success, and satisfaction, as well as staff diversity and fiscal soundness. It must advise college leaders to communicate clearly what the system is expected to accomplish and how the data will be used. The report must advise colleges to provide public disclosure that makes performance assessments understandable to various stakeholders—state policy makers, trustees, faculty, students, community members, and the media. Data should be placed in context, and reports should use nontechnical language and graphic displays that help audiences understand trends and progress in outcomes. Interpretations of the information should be provided when needed.

Consistent leadership. Developing a model for institutional effectiveness takes time and consistent leadership. Unfortunately, the short tenure of college presidents and chancellors in many colleges makes it very difficult for institutions to make progress. Boards of trustees should work to maintain stable leadership and should reinforce the efforts of college chief executive officers by asking for outcome information and by endorsing improvement goals.

New presidents and chancellors need to learn the cultures and values of their institutions. Each institution has its own history and its own strengths and weaknesses, which shape how the institution will define its effectiveness. Processes for reviewing the college mission or establishing a shared vision or strategic plan should be inclusive and representative of all of the college's stakeholders. The final product must be endorsed by all segments of the college community and approved by the board of trustees.

College leaders may experience strong resistance on some fronts; their message may seem to be ignored at times, but they must never give up. The leaders should use every opportunity to communicate and reinforce the student learning mission of the college and the need to be accountable for that mission.

These are challenging times—times when good leadership can make significant differences for colleges and universities. Colleges can choose to proceed along the same path as always, honoring sacred traditions of academia and fighting a continual battle for a larger share of diminishing resources. The alternative is to realize that our colleges must be clearly focused on their missions and must be able to demonstrate their value to the public. Institutional effectiveness information is essential to fulfill that important objective.

BACKGROUND

Palomar College is a public comprehensive community college in southern California. Founded in 1946, the college grew over the years to serve a geographic area of over 2,500 square miles in northern San Diego County. More than 25,000 students enroll in classes each semester in more than 130 different associate degree and certificate programs. In addition to the main San Marcos campus, Palomar College operates eight regional education centers.

The college's open admissions policy and outreach programs encourage enrollment of a diverse student body. A variety of special support programs are offered to enable students to achieve their educational goals. In addition, the college provides worksite education to employees of local businesses and operates a resource center for small business at its Escondido Education Center. Fee-based community services workshops are also scheduled to accommodate the special-interest education needs of local residents.

The college is governed locally by a five-member, publicly elected board of trustees. The president of the Associated Student Government is seated as the student trustee in an advisory capacity. A shared governance plan insures the appropriate involvement of students, faculty, and staff in the development of college policies and procedures. Palomar College is one of the few California community colleges without a unionized faculty.

The Palomar Community College District is one of 71 community college districts in California operating within the guidelines and regulations established by the Chancellor's Office of the California Community Colleges and the Board of Governors, whose members are appointed by the governor of the state. The community colleges in California are accredited by the Accrediting Commission for Community and Junior Colleges of the Western Association of Colleges and Schools. Historically, the California legislature has been very active in regulating the colleges and their practices.

REFERENCES

American Association of Community and Junior Colleges. *Building Communities: A Vision for A New Century*. Washington, DC: AACJC, 1988.

Barker, J.A. *Discovering the Future: The Business of Paradigms*. (2nd ed.) (videotape). Burnsville, MN: Charterhouse International Learning, 1989.

Barkley, C., Mozes, G., Raos, K., and associates. *Institutional Self Study for Reaffirmation of Accreditation*. San Marcos, CA: Palomar College, 1996.

Barr, R. *FactBook 95*. San Marcos, CA: Palomar College, 1995.

Boggs, G.R. "Letter to Colleagues and Friends." *Palomar College 2005: A Shared Vision*. San Marcos, CA: Palomar College, Spring 1991, 1.

Boggs, G.R. *The Year In Review: 1995/96*, San Marcos, CA: Palomar College, 1996.

California Association of Community Colleges. *Indicators and Measures of Successful Community Colleges*. Sacramento, CA: CACC, 1988.

California Association of Community Colleges. *Criteria and Measures of Institutional Effectiveness*. Sacramento, CA: CACC, 1989.

Ewell, P. "Feeling the Elephant: The Quest to Capture 'Quality.'" *Change*, September/October 1992, 44-48.

Far West Laboratories. *Improving It: Accountability By Design*. Sacramento, CA: Chancellor's Office of the California Community Colleges, Contract Number 88-0658, undated.

Giles, R. and Slark, J. "Assessing Institutional Effectiveness." *Trustee Quarterly*, Spring 1989, 2-5.

Nason, J.W. *The Nature of Trusteeship*. Washington DC: Association of Governing Boards, 1982.

O'Banion, T. "A Learning College for the 21st Century." *Community College Journal*, December/January 1995-96, 18-23.

Petersen, J.C. "Assessment in the Western Accrediting Commission for Community and Junior Colleges." *NCA Quarterly*, 65 (2), Fall 1990, 401-402.

Secretary's Commission on Achieving Necessary Skills. *What Work Requires of Schools: A SCANS Report for America 2000*. Washington, DC: U.S. Department of Labor, June 1991.

Senge, P.M. *The Fifth Discipline: The Art and Practice of the Learning Organization*. New York: Doubleday, 1990.

Tagg, J. "It's Time To Put Education On-line." *The San Diego Union-Tribune*, March 9, 1995, B11.

Weldele, C. and associates. *Palomar College Student Equity Plan*. San Marcos, CA: Palomar College, 1995.

Chapter X

There was a young lady of Niger
Who smiled as she rode on a tiger;
They returned from the ride
With the lady inside,
And the smile on the face of the tiger.
—Unknown, *The Young Lady of Niger*

John E. Roueche
Suanne D. Roueche
Community College Leadership Program
The University of Texas at Austin
Laurence F. Johnson
Associate Director
League for Innovation in the Community College
Mission Viejo, California

THE TIGER'S TALE: A NEW STORY FOR COMMUNITY COLLEGES

We began this study with tremendous curiosity about the validity of the current rhetoric that criticizes colleges for their lukewarm, half-hearted responses to increasing calls for improved accountability and institutional effectiveness measures. We intended to determine if and how colleges were responding to public concerns about the quality of their performance. In preparing ourselves to write useful and targeted survey questions, we became intimately familiar with the accountability issues of the past 25 years, especially with the increasing heat created by effectiveness and assessment issues over the past decade.

We concluded that the persistence and intensity of these issues had established clear indicators that the phenomena we were observing were not the particulars of a pendulum swing, but rather of a spiral soar. The issues were not going to go away, nor were the questions and criticisms likely to abate without appropriate and timely college responses. Without doubt, taxpayers, government officials, and accreditation associations have given sufficient notice that demands for educational accountability and effectiveness, and increased scrutiny of the measures by which we and others will judge our performance, will continue to escalate. It is clear that public faith in the capacity of higher education to improve teaching and learning must be restored.

With those concerns and thoughts in mind, we set out to extend prior research and describe the state of the art of the effectiveness movement in two-year colleges in North America. Our primary goal was to draw a realistic picture of institutional effectiveness, of how community colleges are embracing the effectiveness movement, and to what extent they are measuring their own performance. At the very least, using the responses to our effectiveness survey and the experiences of the colleges showcased in the contributed chapters, we believe that this contemporary picture brings the effectiveness issues into sharper focus and assesses the legitimacy of probing, intense criticisms.

From survey responses, we discovered that *while significant steps are being taken by North American community colleges to demonstrate their effectiveness, their progress is decidedly slow.* Apparently, they have earned, legitimately, some of their reputation for timidity and half-hearted attention by their prolonged discussions of viable responses that have few visible links to action and by their unwillingness to do more than meet current minimum standards. We proffer the explanation that perhaps their progress is severely impeded by a critical component in the success of any college initiative and the major unresolved issue identified by survey respondents—staff commitment and willingness to evaluate college practices.

But be that as it may, our survey responses indicate that colleges are not adopting, on any large scale, the basis of the conceptual frameworks most commonly advanced in the literature—that is, tying college mission to expected outcomes. It is evident that the overwhelming majority of colleges are not engaged in data collection activities that would tell them whether or not they are accomplishing their missions. Our survey respondents identified significant problems with such procedural issues as how best to select and design appropriate measures, and how to measure student learning. But for the most part, colleges do not appear to understand (or, perhaps, simply do not know how to make) the critical link between mission and effectiveness. That factor stands squarely in the path of real progress toward assessing institutional effectiveness.

In brief, our survey responses also indicated that, in the majority of colleges, current effectiveness efforts are being driven largely by pressure from funding agencies, regional accrediting associations, and their own boards of trustees. Moreover, tradition continues to play a major role in the selection of effectiveness indicators—such as student degree and completion rates, growth, cost containment, diversity, and transfer number and rate—although colleges now track a larger majority of an expanded list of the 21 most common indicators. Student-learning–related indicators are not routinely tracked although student performance after transfer was identified as an emerging issue. Assessing student academic achievement is a major issue in only one accrediting region; in others, learning-related measures have not yet moved beyond the discussion stage.

Our mix of colleges helped paint the picture of the effectiveness landscape and offered a broad view of large and small, new and old effectiveness practices. They helped us explore strategies in current use that have produced documentable successes and combined theory with practice. Their stories included suggestions and insights, offered process details, described involvement strategies, and identified measurement activities that can inform planning and budgeting. As we stepped back from their individual and unique stories, and looked at them as a collage of effectiveness strategies, we were able to identify a number of common elements woven throughout their messages:

- Clear mission statements that reflect institutional values (values that define the higher education academy itself and the uniqueness of the individual institution) are at the core of all institutional effectiveness strategies (including planning, budgeting, and implementation cycles), and these strategies demand a "custom-fit" design that will reflect the unique characteristics and needs of each college.
- Effectiveness is a process, not an outcome. Developing the process always requires more time than anticipated, and patience is essential.
- The process can be sustained only by cooperation and partnership: the full and consistent support of college leadership and trustees; complete faculty participation in improved teaching and learning; and a viable balance between centrally stimulated action and wide involvement of all individuals who will be affected.
- Data must be: regularly collected; used to improve performance, not to place blame; translated for and into institutional use by credible individuals and groups; and shared with stakeholders in regular and clearly written documents.
- Although applying the complex principles of TQM and CQI to decisionmaking can involve a great deal of labor, time, and training and, many argue, is generally inappropriate for the higher education setting, those who regularly document its successful implementation provide strong support for others of its potential as a "force for good."

We appraised those common elements, examined the issues and initiatives identified in selected contemporary research and criticism, drew several major implications for future discussions of effectiveness, and generated recommendations for colleges. Our recommendations are made within the framework of two overarching questions.

The first is, "Why should colleges respond to calls for viable demonstrations of institutional effectiveness?"

Deciding to respond

Simply speaking, we repeat some common rhetoric of those who support any change and say that colleges must do it to protect themselves, that tena-

cious and intensifying external pressures indicate that is the only choice left
to them; and we also say that they should effect change because it is the right
thing to do. It will help restore public faith in the notion that higher education's best days are not behind it, that the traditional trust the public has
placed in education's ability to improve the common good need not be lost.
And, we would argue further, colleges should demonstrate their effectiveness
because they owe it to their constituencies, the people who pay the bills.

As 1994-95 chairman of the Education Commission of the States,
Colorado Governor Roy Romer observed: "Because higher education is so
important to our future well-being, our investments...must pay high
returns...state leaders...have the responsibility to take steps to ensure [col-
leges] meet our needs and expectations" (Education Commission of the
States, 1995, p. v). External forces are even now doing what they have been
urging colleges to do for more than a decade: they are clarifying their own
expectations for higher education, examining policies and practices to see if
they support these expectations, and developing methods to evaluate how
well colleges meet these expectations by their priorities and services (ECS,
1995, p. 1). And expectations focus squarely on what students are learning
and how well they are learning it. Even a cursory examination of pressures to
examine student learning currently being exerted by a diverse array of external forces clearly indicates that time is of the essence, and it is running out for
colleges who fail to act. States are considering more intrusive measures, writing stricter policies and mandates, and working harder to tie funding to performance—as evidenced by decade-old Tennessee initiatives and others more
recently discussed and enforced in Florida, South Carolina, Kentucky, and
Texas.

Since 1988, when the Department of Education mandated that all accrediting bodies require assessment of the institutions or programs they approve,
increasing numbers of colleges have reported that they conduct internal self-
assessment practices. One recent poll reported as many as 97 percent of all
U.S. colleges implement assessment strategies, most aimed at improving programs and services (Marchese, 1995c). However, concerns that the public
knows too little or may be misinformed about the impact that internal effectiveness measures have on student learning have stirred serious discussions
about the ability of institutions to regulate themselves and about restructuring the present system of accreditation that many pronounce ineffectual and
out of touch. There continue to be strong arguments about what the real problem with accreditation actually is, and lack of agreement about the specific
problem has stymied real progress with what many see as necessary reforms.
They have, in fact, most likely and sadly kept us from trying out any real
alternatives (Marchese, 1995a). However, the discussions continue and
include moving accreditation processes away from an institutional review
that essentially asks colleges to self-report and which may be too "comfy, if

not fishy" (Marchese, 1992, p. 4) toward stronger assessment processes that are genuinely helpful to colleges interested in improvement efforts (Marchese, 1994; Dill, Massy, Wiliams, and Cook, 1996). Proposals for reform efforts include, but are not limited to, internal academic audits, audit trails, and improvement strategies that are monitored by accrediting agencies' external evaluations of the processes by which an individual college assesses its own effectiveness. The discussions are compelling, at first blush, as probable ways in which accrediting agencies can, in reality, perform in the future what they have performed theoretically in the past. However, colleges may have gone beyond the point where the public will support continued self-regulation and accreditation without their involvement (Marchese, 1995a). More and more states now mandate that colleges do for them what accrediting agencies already ask them to do, but "where far more is at stake" (Ewell, 1992, p. 45). With the public's growing lack of confidence in accrediting agencies' abilities (Bogue and Saunders, 1992), their traditional role of assuring the public about the quality of undergraduate education has been seriously weakened and compromised.

In 1995, we saw the rejection of the National Policy Board on Higher Education Institutional Accreditation's proposal for the enforcement of stringent standards for measuring institutional effectiveness through student achievement and the omission of these standards from a subsequent proposal for a new Council for Higher Education Accreditation. This might indicate to many that pressures for quality assurance have disappeared or at least been dramatically reduced, but recent pronouncements by state governors indicate such is not the case. They are, more likely, only in the process of shifting from the federal to the state level (Dill et al., 1996). Examples of serious discussion and actual implementation of performance-based funding policy at the state level are now commonplace—e.g., incentive funding in Colorado, Arkansas' productivity goals, Florida's "rising junior" tests, West Virginia's and South Carolina's "report cards" that threaten to move yet another step toward performance-based funding, and Tennessee's decade-old mandate.

State and public interest in the effectiveness of undergraduate education is not going to go away. There is substantial evidence that both are stronger now than ever before. And more and more frequently, this interest is being endorsed, supported, and aided by organizations and agencies that higher education considers to be its friends—a rather interesting twist to common pronouncement and perceptions that effectiveness is being perpetrated on higher education by meddling legislators. The traditional rhetoric has been that whatever the proposed change under discussion, it must occur because "they"—external agents—will "get us" if it does not happen and that we must make the change before it is done to or in spite of us. It is an uncommon occasion to find that anyone most likely to be affected by the current change has written an article saying that the change should be made for the better-ment of our students or the realization of our own values (Marchese, 1995b, p. 4). Moreover, even individuals and agencies that colleges traditionally have considered to be friends and supporters are calling for assessment reform. Politicians more frequently refer to assessment as a way to effect results from colleges seemingly unwilling to cooperate with requests and wonder, moreover, why "college...leaders don't themselves initiate assess-ment so they can bring better arguments to the table" (Edgerton, 1990, p. 5). Colleges must build the questions that representatives of these entities are asking into the next phases of their work, and they must align their values with the ongoing public-policy conversations about effectiveness indicators (Ewell, 1993).

Getting Better

So we turn to our second overarching question: "How <u>can</u> colleges get better?"

> Unlike the '80s, then, we are running out of opportunities to negoti-ate with society about a mutually agreeable set of standards against which to be held accountable. The task is now different: to actually get better, with the hope that the improvement will be noted in both society's indicators and our own. (Ewell, 1992, p. 46)

Colleges can get better by embracing the effectiveness tiger, acknowledg-ing that the major issues in the debate demand our attention, and creating the most viable plans that can be written in the best interests of the institution and student. They can decide to begin a process of self-renewal, embracing the positive notion of effectiveness as opportunity and refusing to succumb to the debilitating and counterproductive rhetoric of threat.

Overarching recommendations

Colleges should and must begin immediately to respond in timely and appropriate ways to the increasing calls for improved measures of institu-tional effectiveness. No longer can colleges stand back and declare that once they know what effectiveness is they will get about doing it. A decade of description and discussion leaves little to the imagination about what it is. The more widely accepted definitions of effectiveness have been included in this study; common elements that lie just beneath their collective surfaces cre-ate compelling charges and directives for action. Colleges, led by presidents who traditionally set the tone for campus response (Edgerton, 1990), should begin to move immediately to clarify the particulars of the college mission. Comparing results achieved to goals intended (Ewell, 1983) is impossible when the college does not have clear goals and intentions.

> We can know what we are as individuals or as a group only after we have first considered what it is we are trying to become. We can know whether what we are doing is absurd only after we have identified the goals we are trying to achieve. We can know the meaning of our individual jobs only after we have recognized the reason for our coming together as an organization. We are nothing more than what we do, and we can become nothing more than what we see ourselves achieving in terms of goals. (Hughes, 1965, pp. 8-9)

Then college leaders and faculty should set about to determine the most critical activities to which the college should attend (identify critical success factors), to define how the college would know for certain that its mission is being achieved (identify indicators of effectiveness) and to outline a process to improve performance (identify data that will be used to drive decision making—e.g., planning cycles).

Colleges should ensure faculty and administrators are well-informed about the current discussion and action issues of influential policy-making groups and organizations. Rarely does any person or group become excited about effecting change when there is no apparent reason to do so. Only when people agree that a problem exists will they become enthusiastic about solving it. Getting in touch with reality is a must for many who have been relatively sheltered from it. Required reading should become a component of staff and professional development, including documentation of public, legislative, and agency criticisms; and descriptions of successful effectiveness programs. Furthermore, college leadership should move to translate for college constituencies exactly what effects the pressures being brought to bear by these external groups would have on the college and on themselves professionally and personally. In that mix, however, there must be compelling evidence that the leadership will provide the critical support for solving the problems thus identified; everyone in the organization will work toward solutions with more fervor when the college environment is conducive to positive change.

To expedite timely and appropriate responses, colleges should research successful effectiveness practices and make modifications to fit their unique situations. The practices described in the contributed chapters are viable points at which to begin. We purposely did not follow a "best practices" approach, but rather chose to offer an array from the new to the established, the relatively untested practices to those with documentable success. This approach gave us the best opportunity to draw a more useful picture of the realistic diversity of who and where we are after a decade of observing and addressing the effectiveness debate.

There are, as well, a sizable number of successful practices—essentially, within a program of viable college and accreditation agency checks and balances —that have been implemented successfully for a decade or more in foreign institutions of higher education. Descriptions of their rigorous quality-assurance mechanisms hold some promise for North American colleges and accrediting agencies seeking to reform current practice. A major criterion identified within these programs, however, is that a foundation of strong faculty collegiality and shared willingness to evaluate and then improve performance must be in place for the practices to work as they are intended (Roser, 1996). However, given that our survey respondents identified lack of staff commitment and unwillingness to evaluate college practices as a major unresolved issue, we envision that the multiple components of checks and balances—including academic audits, peer reviews, and external audits—will be difficult to sell, much less implement, in our contemporary institutions.

Individuals whose responsibilities and duties will be affected by effectiveness measures should be involved in discussions about evaluation and change. A delicate balance between widespread involvement of multiple constituencies and focused small-group consensus is best achieved by providing various arenas and opportunities for information exchange and decision making. Ample opportunities for candid discussions in informal sessions and formal workgroups and task forces boost participants' confidence that they can influence their environment, reduce the concerns that current problems are not threats but rather are challenges, and promote individual ownership of the final plan of action. Faculty participation is key to improved student learning, and their ownership of a plan of action is critical to its success. While total quality initiatives and continuous quality improvement plans frequently focus on administration, colleges implementing these principles beyond the administrative processes and onto the classroom level report successful integration of faculty into the effectiveness process.

If community colleges believe that the standards by which they are currently being judged are not appropriate—that is, if they could be better used to judge four-year colleges and universities because they ignore substantial differences between institutional types—they must identify and agree in principle upon the major criteria by which they should be judged. How best can colleges respond to mandates? "Either live with them or propose something better—but without an alternative to put on the table, do not expect to fight against them and win" (Ewell, 1992, p. 46). However, not all institutions still have the option of proposing alternatives as state mandates have already been written into policy. But for those colleges who still have the opportunities to propose alternatives, or to impact the mandates being written, must define their own roles and responsibilities before others outside their walls do it totally without their input. There is absolutely no doubt, given the intensity and the volume of concerns, that external forces will broaden and intensify their pressures for broader and more rigid effectiveness measures if colleges do not embrace those currently in place, or do so only in a perfunctory manner. There is substantial evidence that colleges still have some time and opportunity to play significant roles in identifying, shaping, and setting standards by which they will judge themselves and be judged by stakeholders, where they can answer their own questions rather than having to endure circumstances in which assessment will be "'someone else's answers to someone else's questions,'"(Edgerton, 1990, p. 5). Simultaneously, however, there is substantial evidence from existing policy, as well as from public-policy pronouncements and discussions, that both time and opportunity are limited by the public's impatience with current progress and quality of response.

There must be consequences of poor performance or credibility will be lost and the time-consuming and costly effectiveness effort will have been for naught. The courage of the leadership of any college will be tested by evidence of excessive costs; questionable or poor program outcomes; program and service mismatches between funds and mission; and reduced faculty productivity and workloads. Allowed to go unattended, clear violations of the effectiveness plan of action will destroy constituents' confidence that the college is serious about meeting its obligations and will increase concerns about public returns on public investments in higher education. The consequences of poor performance will be played out even more dramatically when performance is tied to funding and already limited funds are further reduced by legislative response to colleges' inattention or reckless disregard for any viable effectiveness program. "Whether higher education itself takes the lead in initiating some form of performance-based funding or we wait for it to be imposed upon us, this approach is going to come into use increasingly around the country" (Ashworth, 1994, p. 11).

Conclusions

Not only is moving toward institutional effectiveness the right thing to do; it is also the only clear-thinking thing left to do. There is no future to riding on the back of the effectiveness tiger; embracing it is higher education's only choice. There are no indications in theory or in practice that the debate or the pressures will subside or disappear. There are indications, however, that they will intensify as concerns worsen about the rising costs of higher education and are juxtaposed with the inefficiencies and shortcomings of the academic enterprise. Virtually every state has accountability mandates and is seriously considering even more intrusive measures. All six accrediting agencies include institutional effectiveness measures within their accreditation standards. The old adage that one should inspect what one expects will be played out in the effectiveness arena. Stakeholders, particularly those who pay the bills, are vitally interested and increasingly discerning about what colleges are and should be doing.

The public has accepted, with surprisingly great patience, the observation that "teaching remains one of the few human activities that does not get demonstrably better from one generation to the next" (Bok, 1992, p.18). But all indications are that its patience has worn thin, if not worn out. Legislators are charging that inefficiency and lack of productivity in higher education should not be rewarded with more support and that rewards should go to institutions that produce the most desirable outcomes and products (Ashworth, 1994). Corporations and individuals, to whom colleges are more frequently turning for donations and other financial supports and partnerships, observe that return on investment will be their major concern: "As [institutions of higher education] look to the private sector more for funding, with that comes expectations; there isn't a business person...who makes a major investment and doesn't follow the dollar and look at performance" (Roser, 1996).

So, for now, colleges that choose to ride rather than embrace the effectiveness tiger risk demonstrating they are not really interested in improving the quality of teaching and learning; or that they are uncertain about their performance and would be embarrassed to share data about what and how much their students are learning; or that they are not concerned about the levels of satisfaction held by their students, transfer institutions, or employers about their programs and services. In effect, they risk sending the message that they do not wish to be nor are they committed to being actively engaged in answering the question: What difference does it make to students and to the larger community that this college is here?

Embracing the tiger requires that colleges step up to the task, as daunting a task as it may be. College administrators and faculty may be steeling themselves to address the debate and the processes by which they must render themselves accountable and effective. Unfortunately, they may feel too much like George S. Kaufman when he lamented in one of his reviews: "I saw the play at a disadvantage; the curtain was up." However, there are colleges whose experiences provide hope and direction for others who are just beginning to embrace the issues of the effectiveness debate or who are being challenged to refine their current plans. For these colleges, there is no public relations problem; there is a performance problem, and they are addressing it. It is their stories of false starts, successes, and failures that will identify the most propitious next steps for others. These times demand the best from institutions that will in fact lose public support and, ultimately, lose faith in themselves, without productive considerations and public demonstrations of "mission accomplished." These times require that colleges get serious about their mission and report regularly and routinely on the extent to which their mission has been accomplished. It is the credible tale of accomplishment the public demands to hear and may well prove to be the best yet for colleges to tell.

REFERENCES

Ashworth, K. "The Texas Case Study: Performance-Based Funding in Higher Education." *Change*, November/December 1994, *26*, 9-15.

Bogue, E.G. and Saunders, R.L. *The Evidence for Quality*. San Francisco: Jossey-Bass, 1992.

Bok, D. "Reclaiming the Public Trust: How Universities and Colleges Need to Cope with a Public Lack of Confidence." *Change*, July/August 1992, *24*, 12-19.

Dill, D.D., Massy, W.F., Williams, P.R., and Cook, C.M. "Accreditation & Academic Quality Assurance: Can We Get There from Here?" *Change*, September/October 1996, *28* 17-24.

Edgerton, R. "Assessment at Half-Time." *Change*, September/October 1990, *22* 4-5.

Education Commission of the States. *Making Quality Count in Undergraduate Education: A Report for the ECS Chairman's "Quality Counts" Agenda in Higher Education*. Denver, CO. Education Commission of the States, 1995.

Ewell, P.T. "The Evidence for Equality" (book review). *Change*, September/October 1992, *24*, 44-47.

Ewell, P.T. *Information on Student Outcomes: How to Get It and How to Use It*. Boulder, CO: National Center for Higher Education Management Services, 1983.

Ewell, P.T. "The Role of States and Accreditors in Shaping Assessment Practice." In Banta, T.W. and associates, *Making a Difference: Outcomes of A Decade of Assessment in Higher Education*. San Francisco, CA: Jossey-Bass, 1993.

Hughes, C.L. *Goal Setting: Key to Individual and Organizational Effectiveness*. New York: American Management Association, 1965.

Marchese, T. "Accreditation—Next Phase" (editorial). *Change*, November/December 1995a, *27*, 4.

Marchese, T. "Getting Smarter About Teaching" (editorial). *Change*, September/October 1995b, *27*, 4.

Marchese, T. "Making a Difference: Outcomes of a Decade of Assessment in Higher Education" (book review). *Journal of Higher Education*, 1995c, *66*, 485-487.

Marchese, T. "Regional Accreditation (II)." *Change*, March/April 1992, *24*, 4.

Marchese, T. "Reinventing Accreditation" (editorial). *Change*, March/April 1994, *26*, 4.

Roser, M.A. "Tenure Faces Biggest Test as Debate Spills Beyond Academe." *Austin American-Statesman*, November 10, 1996, A1, A19.

Appendices

Instructions: Your college has been selected to participate in an international study of institutional effectiveness practices, being conducted by the Community College Leadership Program at The University of Texas at Austin. Confidentiality of all responses is guaranteed, and responses will be reported in summary form. Please check the most appropriate response(s) for each of the items listed.

I. Please identify which of the following indicators your college is currently monitoring. For each indicator *you* are monitoring, please indicate how important you consider this indicator to be in demonstrating your institution's effectiveness.

	Monitoring?		If yes, how important?				
	Yes	No	Not Very	→	→	→	Critical
Student Progress							
Student Goal Attainment	❏	❏	❏	❏	❏	❏	❏
Persistence (Fall to Fall)	❏	❏	❏	❏	❏	❏	❏
Degree/Certificate Completion Rates	❏	❏	❏	❏	❏	❏	❏
Other _____	❏	❏	❏	❏	❏	❏	❏
Career Preparation							
Placement Rate in the Work Force	❏	❏	❏	❏	❏	❏	❏
Employer Assessment of Students	❏	❏	❏	❏	❏	❏	❏
Other _____	❏	❏	❏	❏	❏	❏	❏
Transfer Preparation							
Number and Rate Who Transfer	❏	❏	❏	❏	❏	❏	❏
Performance after Transfer	❏	❏	❏	❏	❏	❏	❏
Other _____	❏	❏	❏	❏	❏	❏	❏
Developmental Education							
Success in Subsequent, Related Coursework	❏	❏	❏	❏	❏	❏	❏
Other _____	❏	❏	❏	❏	❏	❏	❏
General Education							
Demonstration of Critical Literacy Skills	❏	❏	❏	❏	❏	❏	❏
Demonstration of Citizenship	❏	❏	❏	❏	❏	❏	❏
Other _____	❏	❏	❏	❏	❏	❏	❏
Customized Education							
Client Assessment of Programs and Services	❏	❏	❏	❏	❏	❏	❏
Other _____	❏	❏	❏	❏	❏	❏	❏
Community Development							
Responsiveness to Community	❏	❏	❏	❏	❏	❏	❏
Participation Rate in Service Area	❏	❏	❏	❏	❏	❏	❏
Other _____	❏	❏	❏	❏	❏	❏	❏

II. Please identify which of the following indicators are either currently required of your college or under discussion by the listed groups. If any item is not applicable, please leave it blank.

	Board	Funding Agency	Accrediting Agency	Other
Student Progress				
Student Goal Attainment				
Required by:	☐	☐	☐	☐
Under discussion by:	☐	☐	☐	☐
Persistence (Fall to Fall)				
Required by:	☐	☐	☐	☐
Under discussion by:	☐	☐	☐	☐
Degree/Certificate Completion Rates				
Required by:	☐	☐	☐	☐
Under discussion by:	☐	☐	☐	☐
Other _____				
Required by:	☐	☐	☐	☐
Under discussion by:	☐	☐	☐	☐
Career Preparation				
Placement Rate in the Work Force				
Required by:	☐	☐	☐	☐
Under discussion by:	☐	☐	☐	☐
Employer Assessment of Students				
Required by:	☐	☐	☐	☐
Under discussion by:	☐	☐	☐	☐
Other _____				
Required by:	☐	☐	☐	☐
Under discussion by:	☐	☐	☐	☐
Transfer Preparation				
Number and Rate Who Transfer				
Required by:	☐	☐	☐	☐
Under discussion by:	☐	☐	☐	☐
Performance after Transfer				
Required by:	☐	☐	☐	☐
Under discussion by:	☐	☐	☐	☐
Other _____				
Required by:	☐	☐	☐	☐
Under discussion by:	☐	☐	☐	☐
Developmental Education				
Success in Subsequent, Related Coursework				
Required by:	☐	☐	☐	☐
Under discussion by:	☐	☐	☐	☐
Other _____				
Required by:	☐	☐	☐	☐
Under discussion by:	☐	☐	☐	☐
General Education				
Demonstration of Critical Literacy Skills				
Required by:	☐	☐	☐	☐
Under discussion by:	☐	☐	☐	☐
Demonstration of Citizenship Skills				
Required by:	☐	☐	☐	☐
Under discussion by:	☐	☐	☐	☐
Other _____				
Required by:	☐	☐	☐	☐
Under discussion by:	☐	☐	☐	☐

	Board	Funding Agency	Accrediting Agency	Other
Customized Education				
Client Assessment of Programs & Services				
Required by:	❑	❑	❑	❑
Under discussion by:	❑	❑	❑	❑
Other _____				
Required by:	❑	❑	❑	❑
Under discussion by:	❑	❑	❑	❑
Community Development				
Responsiveness to Community Needs				
Required by:	❑	❑	❑	❑
Under discussion by:	❑	❑	❑	❑
Participation Rate in Service Area				
Required by:	❑	❑	❑	❑
Under discussion by:	❑	❑	❑	❑
Other _____				
Required by:	❑	❑	❑	❑
Under discussion by:	❑	❑	❑	❑

III. Please indicate which of the following indicators your college currently monitors. Also indicate how important you consider this indicator to be in demonstrating your institution's effectiveness.

	Monitoring?		If yes, how important?				
	Yes	No	Not Very	→	→	→	Critical
Growth	❑	❑	❑	❑	❑	❑	❑
Cost Containment	❑	❑	❑	❑	❑	❑	❑
Promoting Diversity	❑	❑	❑	❑	❑	❑	❑
Faculty Productivity	❑	❑	❑	❑	❑	❑	❑
Faculty Satisfaction	❑	❑	❑	❑	❑	❑	❑
Staff Productivity	❑	❑	❑	❑	❑	❑	❑
Staff Satisfaction	❑	❑	❑	❑	❑	❑	❑
Use of Indicators/Measures for Planning	❑	❑	❑	❑	❑	❑	❑
Other	❑	❑	❑	❑	❑	❑	❑

IV. Please rank-order the top three of the following according to the influence they currently have on your institution's adoption and use of institutional effectiveness measures.

___Board of Trustees
___Collective Bargaining Agreement(s)
___State/Province/County Legislature
___Regional Accrediting Agency
___State/Province/County Regulatory Agency
___Programmatic Accrediting Agency
___Federal Agency
___Other_____

V. What do you consider the number one issue in institutional effectiveness and outcomes measurement? (Please check only one response.)

❏ Selection and design of appropriate measures
❏ Measurement of student learning
❏ Outcome-based funding
❏ Staff commitment and willingness to evaluate college practices
❏ Other_____

VI. Does your college have a formal, board-approved mission statement?
❏ Yes   ❏ No

If yes, does your college's mission statement include explicit objectives?
❏ Yes   ❏ No

If yes, are these objectives routinely monitored?
❏ Yes   ❏ No

VII. Institutional characteristics. (Please check only one box under each heading.)

Type of Institution
❏ Comprehensive community college
❏ Technical institute
❏ Junior college
❏ Two-year branch of a four-year institution

Organization
❏ Single campus college
❏ College, part of multi-college district
❏ Campus, part of multi-campus district
❏ Other_____

Enrollment
(fall 1995 student headcount in credit courses)
❏ less than 2,500
❏ 2,500-4,999
❏ 5,000-9,999
❏ 10,000-24,999
❏ more than 25,000

Budget
(1995-96 fiscal year)
❏ less than $ 5 million
❏ $ 5-9.9 million
❏ $ 10-19.9 million
❏ $ 20-49.9 million
❏ $ 50 million or more

Location
❏ Urban
❏ Suburban
❏ Rural

Board of Trustees
❏ Elected local board
❏ Appointed local board
❏ State/provincial board

VIII. Please provide the two-letter postal code for your state or province (e.g., CA, TX, ON): _____.

Thank you for completing this survey. Please return by April 15, 1996, to:
Institutional Effectiveness Practices and Directions Survey
John E. Roueche, Sid W. Richardson Regents Chair
Community College Leadership Program, SZB 348
The University of Texas at Austin
Austin, Texas 78712

Appendix B: Survey Letter

March 15, 1996

DATA survey ltr

Dear Salutation:

We invite your participation in a study to determine the extent and extant of institutional effectiveness practices and directions in U.S. and Canadian community colleges. In this new two-part report for the American Association of Community Colleges, we seek (1) to provide rich descriptions of state and accreditation initiatives that are pressing colleges to greater accountability and greater clarity on outcome measures and performance indicators and (2) to feature model college programs that define, describe, and evaluate specific program and college outcomes measures.

The enclosed survey will be the data source for part one of this report. (College) has been selected to help us provide the most hard-hitting, state-of-the-art information about what clearly is "an idea whose time has come." We would greatly appreciate your responses to our queries, helping us better describe the forces that are moving all colleges toward serious improvement of institutional effectiveness policies and practices.

Could you possibly complete this survey and return it to us by April 15? We plan to have the report ready for distribution at the 1997 AACC Convention. Thank you for sharing your best thinking and experiences with us as we prepare this timely snapshot of institutional effectiveness practices, policies, and directions. With every best wish.

Sincerely,

John E. Roueche	Suanne D. Roueche	Larry F. Johnson
Profess and Director	Director, NISOD	Associate Director
Sid W. Richardson Chair	Editor	League for Innovation

JER/SDR/LFJ: rt
Enclosure

About the Authors

John E. Roueche is professor and director of the Community College Leadership Program at The University of Texas at Austin, where he holds the Sid W. Richardson Regents Chair in Community College Leadership. He has served as director of the program since 1971. He is the author of 33 books and more than 150 articles and monographs on the topics of educational leadership and teaching effectiveness. He is the recipient of numerous national awards for his research, teaching, service, and overall leadership, including the 1986 National Distinguished Leadership Award from the American Association of Community Colleges, the 1988 B. Lamar Johnson Leadership in Innovation Award from the League for Innovation in the Community College, and the Distinguished Research Publication Award from the National Association of Developmental Education. He received the 1994 Distinguished Faculty Award at The University of Texas at Austin.

Laurence F. Johnson is executive vice president at Terra Community College, OH, where he serves the multiple roles of chief academic officer, chief student development officer, and chief technology officer. Prior to his current post, he served as associate director of the League for Innovation in the Community College where, working with top corporations and hundreds of community colleges, he developed a series of large-scale research and other projects. As director of the League's Information Technology Initiative, Larry coordinated the world's largest higher education technology conference, the international *Conference on Information Technology*. An author and principal investigator for many national and international studies, he has been recognized for his research by the American Association of Community Colleges and the American Association of University Administrators. He has served on a number of editorial boards, including the *Community College Journal of Research and Practice*, and is the immediate past editor of *Leadership Abstracts*. With 15 years of community college teaching and administrative experience, Larry has been active throughout his career in promoting the understanding of effectiveness practices and has a special interest in the effective application of technology across the range of community college endeavors. Author of a number of books, monographs, and articles, he is much in demand as a speaker and writer in forums across the country.

Suanne D. Roueche is director of the National Institute for Staff and Organizational Development; editor of *Innovation Abstracts*, NISOD's weekly teaching tips publication; editor of *Linkages*, NISOD's quarterly newsletter, and lecturer in the Department of Educational Administration, College of Education, The University of Texas at Austin. Author of more than 12 books and more than 35 articles and book chapters, she is recipient of the 1997 National Leadership Award from the American Association of Community Colleges. She was presented with the 1988

Distinguished Research and Writing Award by the National Council for Staff, Program, and Organizational Development. Suanne and John Roueche received the 1994 Distinguished Senior Scholar Award from AACC's Council of Colleges and Universities for *Between a Rock and a Hard Place: The At-Risk Student in the Open-Door College*. She is the recipient of numerous state and national awards and recognition for her leadership and service, including the "Great Seal of Florida" and The University of Texas at Austin's College of Education Distinguished Service Award. She has been named an Arkansas Traveler, a Kentucky Colonel, and a Yellow Rose of Texas.